JOURNEY TO CUBEVILLE

JOURNEY TO CUBEVILLE

A DILBERT™ BOOK

BY SCOTT ADAMS

Andrews McMeel
Publishing

Kansas City

For Pam "Ah likes to read" Okasaki

Introduction

Rather than fill this page with a frivolous book introduction that you would soon forget, I thought it would be better to answer all of your questions about the nature of the universe. It's more work for me, but you're worth it. Here are the questions I get most often:

Q: I'm a student studying to be an engineer. Is it my fate to sit in a cubicle?

A: No, it's unlikely that you'll be sitting. Recent studies show that if employees are piled like firewood, up to forty can be stored in one cubicle. It's not an ideal arrangement, but you'll get used to it. One thing they don't teach you in school is that you can get used to anything if someone forces you.

Q: Do praying mantises burp?

A: Yes, if they run with their mouths open. That causes huge air pockets to form in their thoraxes, not to mention their boraxes and their pickaxes. That air has to go someplace, otherwise the praying mantis becomes bigger and bigger until eventually it buys dark glasses and becomes Howard Stern. But that only happened once.

Q: Is the planet controlled by a secret society of highly intelligent people?

A: No, we don't like to think of ourselves as a "society." It's more of a cabal. By the way, what was your home address? We'd like to send you something.

Q: Where's the rest of the moon when it's not a full moon?

A: When they landed on the moon in 1969, the astronauts shoveled most of the moon's surface into special containers and took it home. They would have taken the whole thing, but they needed to keep some dirt there to hold the flag up. If you see something that looks like a full moon, that's either a false memory or someone playing a practical joke on you.

I hope that answers all of your questions. If I missed anything, I'll handle it in the next book. In the meantime, if you would like to join the cabal of highly intelligent people, it also goes by the name of Dogbert's New Ruling Class (DNRC). After Dogbert conquers the planet, he'll make everyone outside the DNRC our personal servants. If you're tired of getting up to fetch your own beverages, this is the solution for you. To become a member, all you need to do is put your name on the list to receive the totally free DNRC newsletter, which is published according to the rigorous "whenever I feel like it" schedule. That's about three or four times a year.

To subscribe, send e-mail to listserv@listserv.unitedmedia.com in the following format:

subject: newsletter
message: Subscribe Dilbert_News Firstname Lastname

Don't include any other information—your e-mail address will be picked up automatically.

If the automatic method doesn't work for you, you can also subscribe by writing to scottadams@aol.com or via snail mail:

Dilbert Mailing List
United Media
200 Madison Avenue
New York, NY 10016

These methods are much slower than the automatic method so please be patient.

S.Adams

Scott Adams

DILBERT®

BY **SCOTT ADAMS**

IN THIS TWO DAY WORK-SHOP, YOU WILL LEARN TO EMBRACE OUR COMPANY'S MISSION AND VISION.

AT FIRST GLANCE IT WILL APPEAR TO BE A BUNCH OF USELESS JARGON CREATED BY FUNCTIONALLY ILLITERATE EXECUTIVES.

S. Adams

BUT AFTER WE DO SOME MIND-NUMBING GROUP EXERCISES...

...YOU'LL FORGET THAT YOU'RE UNDERPAID AND YOU HAVE NO JOB SECURITY.

WE'LL BEGIN BY WRITING DOWN ALL THE THINGS THAT "ETHICAL BEHAVIOR" MEANS TO YOU.

I'VE GOT A BETTER IDEA: IF YOU LET US LEAVE NOW, WE'LL GIVE YOU HIGH MARKS ON THE CLASS EVALUATION.

Ethical Behavior

GOOD JOB. YOU TOUCHED ME.

YOU WISH.

WHY DO YOU WANT A JOB AS OUR NETWORK ADMINISTRATOR, MISTER DOGBERT?

I DON'T LIKE PEOPLE. THIS IS A GOOD OPPORTUNITY TO ANNOY IDIOTS SUCH AS YOURSELF FOR MY OWN ENTERTAINMENT.

WOW. YOU'RE PERFECT. CAN YOU START TOMORROW?

SURE, AS FAR AS YOU KNOW. I'LL GIVE YOU MY PAGER NUMBER.

I GOT HIRED AS THE NETWORK ADMINISTRATOR FOR YOUR COMPANY.

HERE'S MY CARD. YOU CAN ONLY REACH ME BY E-MAIL OR BY PAGER.

WHEN THE NETWORK BREAKS, NO E-MAIL. I'LL JUST SIT AROUND AND WAG MY TAIL.

YOUR PAGER NUMBER HAS A TILDE... HOW DO I DIAL A TILDE?

NETWORK ADMINISTRATOR

I HAVE TOTAL ACCESS TO EVERY EMPLOYEE'S E-MAIL MESSAGES.

WITH A FEW STRATEGIC EDITS I WILL TRANSFORM THE OFFICE INTO "MELROSE PLACE."

YES, ALICE... I WILL BE YOUR "MONKEY OF LOVE."

NETWORK ADMINISTRATOR

I HAVE FORGOTTEN MY PASSWORD. I HUMBLY BEG FOR ASSISTANCE.

I HAVE NO TIME FOR BORING ADMINISTRATIVE TASKS, YOU FOOL! I'M BUSY UPGRADING THE NETWORK!

YOU COULD HAVE GIVEN ME A NEW PASSWORD IN THE TIME IT TOOK TO BELITTLE ME.

YES, BUT WHICH OPTION WOULD GIVE ME JOB SATISFACTION?

AS NETWORK ADMINISTRATOR I CAN TAKE DOWN THE NETWORK WITH ONE KEYSTROKE.

AAGH!!! WAAA!!!
AEEE!!
EEEK!!
MY WORK!!

IT'S JUST LIKE BEING A DOCTOR BUT WITHOUT GETTING GOOKY STUFF ON MY PAWS.

THE NETWORK ADMINISTRATOR

CAN YOU PROGRAM THE ROUTERS TO BLOCK EMPLOYEES FROM ALL FUN WEB SITES?

WHY STOP THERE? I CAN PROGRAM THE ROUTERS TO BLOCK ALL USELESS ACTIVITIES.

HOW LONG WILL THAT TAKE?

DONE.

I'VE SEEN YOUR BUSINESS PLAN.

Poink

DILBERT

BY
SCOTT ADAMS

TINA, WE NEED A FEW MINOR EDITS ON OUR PRODUCT BROCHURE.

MINOR? UH-OH...

WE'VE DISCOVERED THAT OUR PRODUCT CAUSES HALLUCINATIONS AND STERILITY.

SEE IF YOU CAN PUT A POSITIVE SPIN ON THAT.

THIS WILL BE MY GREATEST WRITING CHALLENGE YET.

"ARE YOU TIRED OF THE SAME OLD SIGHTS? WE'VE GOT YOU COVERED."

"... MAKES A GREAT GIFT FOR THOSE PEOPLE WHO — IN YOUR OPINION — SHOULD NOT REPRODUCE."

OOH... I FEEL A TINY PANG OF CONSCIENCE.

THAT'S ONE.

SO THE BROCHURE WAS ONLY A THREE-PANGER?

YEAH, AND I THINK I FAKED THE THIRD ONE.

MR. CATBERT, OUR EVIL DIRECTOR OF HUMAN RESOURCES, WILL DESCRIBE OUR NEW CUBICLE PLAN.

LAST YEAR WE REDUCED THE SIZE OF CUBICLES IN THE DENSIFICATION PROJECT.

WE DIDN'T SAVE MUCH MONEY, BUT WE DID LOWER MORALE.

THIS YEAR WE'LL BUILD ON THAT SUCCESS...

WITH THE PATENTED "HEAD CUBICLE."

HOLD STILL, WALLY.

AND THE HEAD CUBICLE CAN BE RECYCLED AFTER YOU'RE DOWNSIZED!

WE REALLY NEED TO DRAW THE LINE AT SOME POINT.

WHILE WE STILL HAVE OUR DIGNITY.

ON WEEKENDS I'LL FEEL MY PAGER VIBRATE... BUT WHEN I GO TO CHECK IT, I REALIZE I'M NOT WEARING IT.

IT'S A CLASSIC CASE OF PHANTOM-PAGER SYNDROME. IT'S COMMON AMONG TECHNOLOGY WORKERS.

THERE'S NO TREATMENT FOR IT.

I DON'T WANT TO TREAT IT. I WANT TO RELOCATE IT.

WHEN THE YEAR 2000 COMES, YOUR COMPUTERS WILL THINK IT'S THE YEAR "OO" AND CAUSE MAJOR PROBLEMS.

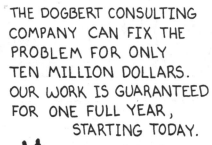

THE DOGBERT CONSULTING COMPANY CAN FIX THE PROBLEM FOR ONLY TEN MILLION DOLLARS. OUR WORK IS GUARANTEED FOR ONE FULL YEAR, STARTING TODAY.

BUT WHY WOULD I CARE? THE YEAR "OO" IS BEFORE I'M BORN.

AMAZING... YOU'D ACTUALLY HAVE TO BE **SMARTER** TO DO SOMETHING **STUPID**.

RATBERT, YOUR JOB IS TO REVIEW EIGHTY MILLION LINES OF COMPUTER CODE IN THE COMPANY'S SYSTEMS.

YOU'RE LOOKING FOR ANY REFERENCE TO THE CURRENT YEAR. THOSE PIECES OF CODE WILL BE A PROBLEM WHEN THE YEAR IS 2000.

GOTCHA

SIX MONTHS LATER

I'M HAPPY TO REPORT THAT THE DATE DID NOT SHOW UP ONCE. IN FACT, IT WAS ALL JUST ZEROS AND ONES!

OOPS.

16

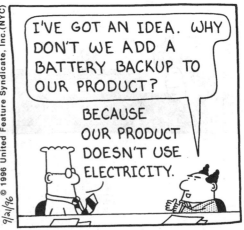

I DON'T KNOW HOW TO FIX ANY OF THE PROBLEMS IN THIS COMPANY. MAYBE I'LL JUST SIT HERE QUIETLY.

NO, THAT WOULDN'T LOOK MANAGERLY... I'LL HAVE TO DO SOMETHING IDIOTIC AND HOPE IT LOOKS LIKE LEADERSHIP.

WE'RE GOING TO HAVE AN "IRON MAN" TEAM-BUILDING COMPETITION.

WHAT A BUNCH OF LEADERSHIP...

MY BOSS IS MAKING THE ENGINEERS COMPETE IN AN "IRON MAN" EVENT. IT'S SUPPOSED TO IMPROVE TEAMWORK.

I'M GLAD I TAKE THE STAIRS SOMETIMES INSTEAD OF USING THE ELEVATOR. I'M IN PRETTY GOOD SHAPE.

YES, YOU ARE, TO THE EXTENT POTATO IS A PRETTY GOOD SHAPE.

I JUST WRENCHED A MUSCLE.

THE FIRST LEG OF THE "IRON MAN" TEAM-BUILDING EXERCISE IS A TEN-MILE SWIM, I THINK.

I WON'T BE PARTICIPATING BECAUSE MY TEAMWORK SKILLS ARE ALREADY EXCELLENT.

TWO PHRASES YOU DON'T EXPECT TO HEAR IN THE SAME DAY ARE "IRON MAN" AND "DOGGIE PADDLE."

HEY! NO SPLASHING!

THE TEAM-BUILDING EXERCISE

UH-OH... I'M A MILE FROM SHORE AND TOO EXHAUSTED TO SWIM BACK.

MY ONLY HOPE IS THAT AN INTELLIGENT DOLPHIN WILL SEE MY PLIGHT AND RESCUE ME.

I'M IN LUCK!

TWO WORDS: TUNA...NET.

SOME DOLPHINS IN MY SITUATION WOULD HELP YOU GET TO SHORE SAFELY.

OTHERS MIGHT TRY TO DISTRACT YOU WHILE AN ACCOMPLICE PLAYED A CRUEL JOKE.

COME BACK HERE WITH MY TRUNKS!!!

LET'S ASK THE HUMMING FISH TO DO THE "JAWS" THEME SONG.

...THERE I WAS, NAKED AND EXHAUSTED, MILES FROM SHORE. DOLPHINS TAUNTED ME FOR HOURS.

SUDDENLY A DEEP SEA SPORT FISHING BOAT HAPPENED BY. I GRABBED THE LINE AND HELD ON FOR MY LIFE.

WOW! THAT'S LUCKY.

THAT'S WHAT I THOUGHT... UNTIL THE SECOND TIME THEY THREW ME BACK IN.

I MEANT LUCKY FOR THEM.

DILBERT

BY **SCOTT ADAMS**

GROAN.

ACCOUNTING

I SAVED $500 IN AIRFARE BY EXTENDING MY BUSINESS TRIP TO SATURDAY.

WHY WON'T YOU REIMBURSE ME FOR THE SATURDAY HOTEL COSTS?

SATURDAY WAS NOT A BUSINESS-RELATED ACTIVITY.

HMM... LET ME SEE IF I UNDERSTAND THIS...

IT'S **NOT** BUSINESS-RELATED TO MAKE SENSIBLE ECONOMIC CHOICES...

BUT IT **IS** BUSINESS-RELATED TO WASTE MONEY LIKE AN UGLY, BRAIN-DEAD TROLL...

THEN HE BEAT ME UP AND TOOK MY LUNCH MONEY.

ARE YOU SAYING I CAN GET FREE LUNCH MONEY BY BEATING YOU UP?

CATBERT, EVIL H.R. DIRECTOR

I NEED TO HIRE A PROGRAMMER FOR MY PROJECT TEAM.

OUR POLICY IS TO FIRST SEEK CANDIDATES FROM WITHIN THE COMPANY. IF NONE IS QUALIFIED, YOU MUST USE A SOCK PUPPET.

HOW MANY OF YOUR POLICIES ARE DESIGNED FOR THE SOLE PURPOSE OF SATISFYING YOUR SADISTIC TENDENCIES?

ALL OF THEM. SOME ARE JUST MORE OBVIOUS.

WE'LL BE HAVING AN ISO 9000 AUDIT SOON. THEY'LL CHECK TO SEE IF WE FOLLOW OUR OWN DOCUMENTED PROCEDURES FOR EVERYTHING WE DO.

I'VE DIVIDED OUR PREPARATION TASKS INTO TWO GROUPS: UNETHICAL AND UNPRODUCTIVE.

I'LL TRAIN OUR DEPARTMENT TO LIE TO THE AUDITOR. YOU CAN DOCUMENT OUR INANE PROCEDURES.

NO FAIR. YOU DID UNETHICAL LAST TIME TOO!

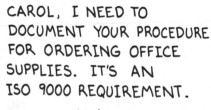

CAROL, I NEED TO DOCUMENT YOUR PROCEDURE FOR ORDERING OFFICE SUPPLIES. IT'S AN ISO 9000 REQUIREMENT.

IF SOMEONE ASKS FOR SOMETHING, I CHECK THE SUPPLY CABINET FIRST. THEN I SAY, "THERE'S ONE LEFT. YOU CAN'T HAVE IT BECAUSE THEN WE'D BE ALL OUT."

THEN I SPEND THE REST OF THE DAY COMPLAINING ABOUT THE PERSON WHO ASKED.

UH-OH... I'M OUT OF INK.

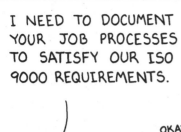
I NEED TO DOCUMENT YOUR JOB PROCESSES TO SATISFY OUR ISO 9000 REQUIREMENTS.

OKAY.

I TRY TO ANTICIPATE THE SHIFTING POLITICAL WINDS. THEN I WRAP MYSELF IN THE RELEVANT BUZZWORDS AND TRY TO ACHIEVE IMPORTANCE WITHOUT ADDING VALUE.

WHAT'S YOUR JOB TITLE?

DIRECTOR OF ISO 9000 QUALITY PROCESS DESIGN.

YOUR PRODUCT LOOKS GOOD, BUT YOU CAN'T BE OUR SUPPLIER UNLESS YOUR COMPANY IS ISO 9000 CERTIFIED.

SO... YOU DON'T CARE HOW BAD OUR INTERNAL PROCESSES ARE, AS LONG AS THEY'RE WELL-DOCUMENTED AND USED CONSISTENTLY?

THAT'S RIGHT.

OUR DOCUMENTED PROCESS SAYS I MUST NOW LAUGH IN YOUR FACE AND DOUBLE OUR PRICE.

YOU KNOW WHAT'S FUNNY?

I'LL TELL YOU.

YOU'RE WORKING HARD. I'M DOING NOTHING. IN A HUNDRED YEARS WE'LL BOTH BE DEAD.

YOU MIGHT NOT NEED TO WAIT THAT LONG.

I THINK I'LL SPREAD SOME JOY OVER THIS WAY.

DILBERT®
BY
SCOTT ADAMS

NOBODY HAS NOMINATED A CO-WORKER FOR A SPECIAL ACHIEVEMENT AWARD.

SOMEONE IN THIS GROUP MUST HAVE DONE **SOMETHING** GOOD THIS YEAR.

NO... I DON'T THINK SO.

WE'D REMEMBER SOMETHING LIKE THAT.

THIS LOOKS BAD. ALL THE OTHER DEPARTMENTS ARE GIVING THEMSELVES AWARDS.

WE MIGHT HAVE TO LOWER OUR STANDARDS A BIT.

I'VE BEEN PROACTIVE IN THAT AREA.

WHY ARE WE STANDING IN THE HALLWAY?

WE THINK THE ROOM IS LOCKED.

WE DON'T HAVE THE KEY.

LATER THAT MONTH

THIS AWARD GOES TO ALICE FOR BOLDLY TRYING THE DOOR KNOB.

WHEN I FIND OUT WHO NOMINATED ME...

© 1996 United Feature Syndicate, Inc.

24

ALICE, I'M PUTTING YOU IN CHARGE OF DEVELOPING OUR BOOTH FOR THE BIG TRADE SHOW.

I PICKED YOU BECAUSE THE MALES IN THE DEPARTMENT HAVE DISQUALIFIED THEMSELVES THROUGH A PROCESS OF STRATEGIC INCOMPETENCE.

WHAT IS STRATEGIC INCOMPETENCE?

I HAD THAT WRITTEN DOWN SOMEPLACE, BUT I LOST IT.

IF YOU PLAN TO HAVE A BOOTH AT THE TRADE SHOW, YOU NEED THE "DOGBERT TRADE-SHOW CONSULTING COMPANY" TO DESIGN IT.

I RECOMMEND THE DELUXE BOOTH. IT'S GUARANTEED TO GENERATE THE MOST REVENUE.

HOW WOULD THE DELUXE BOOTH GENERATE MORE REVENUE FOR MY COMPANY?

OH, SUDDENLY THIS IS ABOUT YOUR COMPANY?

YOUR BOOTH AT THE TRADE SHOW MUST BE ATTENTION-GRABBING. YOU HAVE SEVERAL OPTIONS.

1. MAGIC TRICKS
2. SPECIAL EFFECTS
3. RAFFLES
4. BOOTH BABES

FOR THE BEST RESULT, COMBINE ALL FOUR: CREATE THE ILLUSION THAT YOU'RE RAFFLING OFF THE BOOTH BABES.

BOOTH BABES?

DILBERT
BY SCOTT ADAMS

MY PROJECT IS RIGHT ON PLAN.

IT BEGAN LAST WEEK AS A BAD IDEA FROM SOMEBODY IN SENIOR MANAGEMENT.

THANKS TO MY LEADERSHIP, IT IS ALREADY AN OBJECT OF WIDESPREAD MOCKERY AND DERISION.

AS I SPEAK, OUR LAWYERS ARE PURGING EVERY LAST TRACE OF VALUE IT MIGHT HAVE HAD.

WITH LUCK, THE PROJECT WILL BE A GIGANTIC FAILURE IN A MONTH.

PEOPLE WILL FORGET MY FAILURE AND REMEMBER THAT I'M EXPERIENCED. PROMOTIONS WILL FOLLOW.

YES!!

IN SIX MONTHS I'LL BE DATING AN EXECUTIVE SECRETARY NAMED YVONNE.

GOOD PLAN.

WALLY, HAVE YOU EVER READ OUR MISSION STATEMENT?

YEAH, BUT I DON'T SUBSCRIBE TO A LITERAL INTERPRETATION.

ON THE SURFACE, YOU SEEM TO MAKE SOME GOOD POINTS ABOUT TECHNOLOGY...

CLICK CLICK CLICK

BUT YOUR E-MAIL ADDRESS REVEALS YOUR NEWBIE IDENTITY. YOU'RE PROBABLY A GOAT HERDER OR A CARTOONIST.

CLICK CLICK CLICK

HOW DOES IT FEEL TO BE AN ELITIST TECHNOLOGY BIGOT?

I PREFER TO THINK OF MYSELF AS A TECHNOLOGY "HAVE."

THANKS FOR THE MEETING. HERE'S MY CARD.

YOU CALL THAT AN E-MAIL ADDRESS? IT'S EIGHTY CHARACTERS LONG AND MOSTLY MEANINGLESS.

PEOPLE WITH EMBARRASSING E-MAIL SYSTEMS...

I TELL PEOPLE, "THE REPLY FUNCTION DOESN'T WORK. YOU HAVE TO TYPE IN MY ADDRESS."

LOSER.

CATBERT: EVIL H.R. DIRECTOR

I FEEL LIKE COMMITTING RANDOM ACTS OF CATNESS.

WOMAN IN PINK SUIT APPROACHING ... ACTIVATE PURRING AND SHEDDING.

PURR PURR PURR

SO, ALICE, HOW LONG DOES IT TAKE TO CURL AND STYLE A SUIT LIKE THAT?

DO YOU DRY-CLEAN IT OR JUST GIVE IT A PERM?

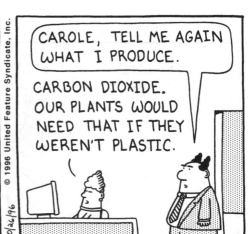

DILBERT

BY SCOTT ADAMS

ALICE, I'D LIKE YOU TO MEET THE NEWEST MEMBER OF MY MANAGEMENT TEAM.

KEITH IS HIGHLY QUALIFIED. HE HAS A MASTERS IN BUSINESS ADMINISTRATION.

VERY IMPRESSIVE. THEY MUST HAVE TAUGHT YOU A LOT ABOUT MOTIVATING EMPLOYEES.

NO, NOT REALLY.

WELL... YOU PROBABLY LEARNED HOW TO IDENTIFY AND HIRE GOOD PEOPLE, RIGHT?

THAT MIGHT HAVE BEEN OPTIONAL READING.

DID YOU LEARN NEGOTIATION SKILLS?

STRATEGIC THINKING?

BUSINESS WRITING?

NO.
NO.
NO.

IT WAS MOSTLY FINANCE AND ACCOUNTING.

AND ECONOMICS.

SO, YOU'RE A HIGHLY QUALIFIED LEADER BECAUSE ... YOU'RE GOOD AT MATH?

WHAT SHOULD I DO HERE?

IN THESE SITUATIONS I LIKE TO USE SWEARING.

THE DOGBERT CONSULTING COMPANY WILL ADD CREDIBILITY TO YOUR OWN SELFISH AND IDIOTIC OPINIONS.

FOR EXAMPLE, YOUR CURRENT BUDGET SHOULD BE... UM...

DOUBLED

DOUBLED. IT SHOULD BE DOUBLED.

HEY, WHAT'S THAT TINGLE I FEEL ALL OVER MY BODY?!!

CREDIBILITY. IF YOU WANT ANOTHER HIT, IT'LL COST YOU.

I HIRED THE DOGBERT CONSULTING COMPANY TO ADD CREDIBILITY TO MY DECISIONS.

AS MY ANALYSIS SHOWS, IT'S MUCH BETTER TO GIVE YOUR MONEY TO ME THAN TO WASTE IT ON FUTURE DOWNSIZEES SUCH AS YOURSELVES.

WHAT ANALYSIS? THIS IS A PAGE RIPPED OUT OF THE MAGAZINE IN OUR LOBBY.

PERHAPS YOU SHOULD UPGRADE TO MY DELUXE SERVICE.

I'VE DECIDED TO DATE OTHER MEN.

NOOO!!! DON'T BREAK UP WITH ME!

I'M NOT. I JUST WANT TO DATE OTHER MEN AT THE SAME TIME.

I AM **NOT** HAPPY RIGHT NOW.

THAT'S EXACTLY WHY I NEED A SPARE.

LIZ STARTED DATING OTHER MEN. TWO CAN PLAY AT THAT GAME.

I WILL USE THE POWER OF THE INTERNET TO FIND A HOT BABE.

AH! HERE'S ONE.

SHE WANTS YOUR CREDIT CARD NUMBER.

OOH! SHE'S INQUISITIVE. I LIKE THAT.

MEN WHO UNDERSTAND TECHNOLOGY ARE THE NEW SEX SYMBOLS. YOUR ONLINE PERSONALS AD SHOULD EMPHASIZE YOUR TECHNICAL PROWESS.

HOW ABOUT "LOOKING FOR WOMAN WHO LIKES MOONLIT WALKS SO I'LL HAVE MORE TIME ALONE WITH MY COMPUTER"?

AND "MUST LIKE TO DANCE." THAT'S SO I WON'T GET A FLABBY, UNCOORDINATED APPLICANT.

DON'T CALL THEM "APPLICANTS" ON THE FIRST DATE.

YOU HAVE TO MOVE SLOWLY WITH THESE ONLINE RELATIONSHIPS. I'LL ASK HER WHAT SHE LIKES TO DO FOR FUN.

YIPE!

YOU'D THINK THAT A WOMAN NAMED MADAME CRUELLA WOULD COMPENSATE BY BEING EXTRA NICE.

CATBERT: EVIL H.R. DIRECTOR

THERE ARE TWO WAYS TO GET AN EXTRA ENGINEER FOR YOUR PROJECT.

YOU CAN TRANSFER SOME UNQUALIFIED LOSER FROM WITHIN THE COMPANY...

OR?

NOT SO FAST. I LIKE TO SAVOR THE MOMENT BEFORE I CRUSH YOUR MISPLACED OPTIMISM.

CATBERT: EVIL H.R. DIRECTOR

HERE ARE THE RÉSUMÉS OF HIGHLY QUALIFIED APPLICANTS FOR YOUR OPENING.

IT'S TOO BAD WE DON'T PAY ENOUGH TO HIRE QUALIFIED APPLICANTS. HA HA HA HA HA HA!!

ZIP

LET'S SEE... WE'VE GOT RÉSUMÉS IN PENCIL... CRAYON...PENCIL... EYELINER...

HEY! DOT MATRIX!

WE LIKE TO ASK OUR APPLICANTS SOME QUESTIONS THAT WILL ALLOW US TO SEE HOW YOU THINK.

IF YOU HAVE A FIVE-GALLON BUCKET AND A FIFTY-GALLON BUCKET, HOW CAN YOU TELL WHICH ONE HOLDS MORE WATER?

WHEN I SAID, "SEE HOW YOU THINK," WHAT I MEANT WAS...

OW! OW! OW!

DILBERT

BY SCOTT ADAMS

THE POWERFUL LEADER ENTERS CUBEVILLE TO INSPIRE THE WRETCHED UNDERLINGS.

HE SPOTS ONE OF THE LITTLE PEOPLE IN DESPERATE NEED OF A MORALE BOOST.

THE LEADER CAREFULLY ASSESSES THE SITUATION. EVERY SOLUTION IS UNIQUE.

TRY IDENTIFYING THE PROBLEM AND THEN SOLVING IT.

THE LEADER WAITS WHILE THE BRILLIANCE OF HIS CONTRIBUTION SINKS IN.

THAT'S A MUCH BETTER IDEA THAN WHAT I WAS DOING.

I'VE BEEN SITTING HERE ALL DAY RANDOMLY PRESSING KEYS. BUT YOU'VE SHOWN ME A BETTER WAY!

SUDDENLY THE LEADER REMEMBERS WHY HE RARELY VISITS CUBEVILLE.

MY MORALE IS SOARING.

CATBERT, EVIL H.R. DIRECTOR

ARE YOU STRESSED OUT, WALLY? I HAVE A SOLUTION.

START SMOKING. THAT WAY YOU'LL HAVE FREQUENT COMPANY-SANCTIONED BREAKS THROUGHOUT THE DAY.

THIS IS YOUR STRATEGY FOR DOWN-SIZING, ISN'T IT?

TRY IT, YOU BIG WUSS.

I'VE DECIDED TO START SMOKING. I'LL BE ABLE TO TAKE MORE BREAKS THAT WAY.

AND FRANKLY, I'M HOPING IT WILL ADD AN INTERESTING EDGE TO MY PERSONALITY AND HELP ME SOCIALLY.

NOT THAT I NEED ANY HELP.

I CAN ONLY PRAY THAT YOUR PERSONAL MAGNETISM WON'T ERASE MY HARD DRIVE.

HERE'S MY FIRST CIGARETTE EVER. I'M LOOKING FORWARD TO THE MANY SMOKING BREAKS I'M ENTITLED TO.

I'LL PROBABLY SEE YOU THREE TIMES A DAY, JUST SMOKING AND CHATTING AND ENJOYING THE FRESH AIR!

I ASSUME YOU LIGHT THE COLOR-CODED END, RIGHT?

I QUIT.

44

DILBERT® BY SCOTT ADAMS

LAST WEEK OUR CONSULTANTS WARNED US ABOUT A SERIOUS THREAT.

THEY SAID OUR COMPETITORS WOULD "EAT OUR LUNCH."

EAT OUR LUNCH

I'M HAPPY TO TELL THE EXECUTIVE COMMITTEE THAT I LEAPT INTO ACTION.

I HIRED A SECURITY GUARD TO PROTECT THE CAFETERIA.

OUR LUNCHES ARE SAFE.

I ALWAYS THOUGHT THAT WAS JUST A FIGURE OF SPEECH.

FOOL! GIVE ME YOUR DEPARTMENT!

LET GO OF MY HAIR!!

SLAP

OUCH!!

THIS IS GOING BETTER THAN USUAL.

WHY IS THE CAFETERIA CLOSED?

SOMEONE ATE ALL THE LUNCHES.

BURP

THIS LESSON IN INTER-
PERSONAL SKILLS INVOLVES
LISTENING TO A STUPID
PERSON WITHOUT ROLLING
YOUR EYES.

MY COMPUTER SCREEN
SAYS, "PRESS ANY
KEY TO CONTINUE."
CAN I BORROW YOUR
KEYS? MINE
ARE LOCKED IN
MY YUGO.

MUST
FOCUS...
MUST...
FOCUS...

I COULD BREAK
THE DRIVER'S SIDE
WINDOW... BUT
IT'S BAD ENOUGH
THAT THE WIND-
SHIELD IS GONE.

HERE'S MY PRESENTATION
PACKAGE. I WORKED
TWELVE STRAIGHT HOURS
ON IT.

THAT INCLUDES THREE
HOURS OF CREATIVITY
FOLLOWED BY NINE HOURS
OF STUPOR, SENSELESS
TWIDDLING AND OUT-
RIGHT DEMENTIA.

I SUPPOSE THERE'S ONLY
ONE THING THAT COULD
MAKE THIS PRESENTATION
WORSE.

SEND IT
AROUND
FOR
COMMENTS.

I FOUND MANY AREAS
FOR IMPROVEMENT IN
YOUR DOCUMENT, ALICE.

I'M ONLY AN INTERN,
BUT THESE ERRORS
STAND OUT LIKE HUGE,
RED, BLINKING LIGHTS.

YOU COULD
PUT THIS
ON TOP OF
AN AMBU-
LANCE AS
A WARNING.

I WAS
THINKING
THE SAME
THING
ABOUT YOU.

 THIS METRIC SHOWS AN EXCELLENT TREND IN THE NUMBER OF DAYS SINCE THE BEGINNING OF MY PROJECT.

 THAT GROWTH RATE COMPARES FAVORABLY WITH THE BEST COMPANIES IN OUR TIME ZONE.

 I'M WORKING SMARTER, NOT HARDER.

IT'S A WHOLE NEW PARADIGM.

 I'M GOING TO ENTER A PROFESSION THAT WILL MAKE A HUGE DIFFERENCE IN MY SELF-ESTEEM.

 I'LL BE A CORPORATE TRAINER IN A COMPANY THAT'S DOWNSIZING.

ARE YOU SURE THAT WILL RAISE YOUR SELF-ESTEEM?

WHY WOULD I WANT TO RAISE IT?

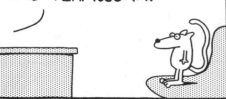 I'M LOOKING FOR A NEW CORPORATE TRAINER TO HELP ME TEACH CLASSES IN STRESS REDUCTION, CONFLICT RESOLUTION, AND TEAMWORK.

 I'LL BURN IN HELL BEFORE I'LL DO YOUR WORK PLUS MY OWN, YOU FILTHY WEASEL!!!

AND THEY HIRED YOU?

A GOOD TRAINER DOESN'T HAVE TO BE A SUBJECT MATTER EXPERT.

RATBERT, CORPORATE TRAINER

PSSST!

I'M THE GRIM DOWNSIZER. TRAINERS ARE THE FIRST TO GO. I'LL JUST HANG AROUND HERE UNTIL THE NEXT BUDGET CUTS.

DO YOU MIND IF I SIT IN ON YOUR STRESS-REDUCTION CLASS?

I DON'T THINK I'LL READ THE CLASS EVALUATION FORMS FROM THIS ONE.

RATBERT: CORPORATE TRAINER

LET'S GO AROUND THE ROOM AND SAY WHO WE ARE AND WHAT WE HOPE TO GET OUT OF THE CLASS.

I'M THE GRIM DOWNSIZER. I'M HERE TO DECRUIT THE ENTIRE TRAINING DEPARTMENT PLUS ALL OF THE PEOPLE WHO HAVE TIME TO ATTEND CLASSES.

MY NAME IS DILBERT. I'M HERE IN PLACE OF WALLY WHO IS WORKING HARD TO BUILD A BETTER TOMORROW.

NICE TRY.

I'M SOMEBODY ELSE TOO.

YOU'RE BEING DOWNSIZED, RATBERT. FORTUNATELY, THERE'S A GENEROUS RETIREMENT PLAN.

LET'S SEE... FOR YOUR LENGTH OF EMPLOYMENT, AT YOUR GRADE LEVEL... YOU GET A WALL CALENDAR.

WHEN DO I GET IT?

AS SOON AS I'M DONE WITH IT.

DILBERT

BY SCOTT ADAMS

CATBERT, EVIL H.R. DIRECTOR

THE MANDATORY UNPAID OVERTIME IS IMMORAL. IT'S DESTROYING THE QUALITY OF MY LIFE.

ALICE, ALICE, ALICE... COMPANIES ARE DESIGNED TO MAXIMIZE STOCKHOLDER VALUE, NOT EMPLOYEE HAPPINESS.

MAYBE THE HEAD OF HUMAN RESOURCES SHOULD BE A HUMAN.

PRIVATELY I REFER TO MYSELF AS THE DIRECTOR OF DISGRUNTLED CAT TOYS.

DOGBERT THE CONSULTANT

LET ME DO THE TALKING WHEN WE MEET WITH YOUR BOSS.

AS YOU KNOW, ANY IDEA FROM THE POINTY-HAIRED WONDER IS CRUD, BUT WHEN YOU ADD MY ABILITY, WHAT DO YOU HAVE?

CRUDABILITY?

AND GOOD LOOKS TOO!

YOUR FIRST DRAFT WAS BORING, SO I ADDED A BUNCH OF EXCLAMATION POINTS.

WOW! THOSE EXCLAMATION POINTS MAKE THIS TECHNICAL DOCUMENT COME ALIVE!

THIS MIGHT BE THAT SARCASM THING I KEEP HEARING ABOUT.

I'M IN THE PRESENCE OF GENIUS! I BEG YOU TO FATHER MY CHILDREN!

DILBERT
BY
SCOTT ADAMS

I MADE AN UPGRADE TO YOUR PRODUCT DESIGN.

THIS WOULD MAKE THE PRODUCT OVERHEAT.

LET'S TRY TO LOOK AT THE BIG PICTURE.

OKAY... LET'S SEE ...

YOUR UPGRADE HAS NO BENEFITS AND IT COSTS MORE.

THE OVERHEATING WOULD START OFFICE FIRES AND PUT ALL OF OUR CUSTOMERS OUT OF BUSINESS.

IF OUR SALES ARE STRONG, WE COULD CREATE ECONOMIC CHAOS AND A GLOBAL FIRESTORM.

YOUR "UPGRADE" WOULD DESTROY CIVILIZATION AS WE KNOW IT.

KEEP ME INFORMED.

SO YOU'RE GOING TO END CIVILIZATION AS WE KNOW IT?

I DON'T THINK I'LL MISS IT, FRANKLY.

AS A CONSULTANT, I EARN $150 PER HOUR EVEN WHEN I'M UNPRODUCTIVE.

I CAN EARN 42 CENTS BY WIGGLING MY FURRY LITTLE BEHIND FOR TEN SECONDS.

C'MON, COUNT WITH ME !!!

WHEN I IMAGINE MY IDEAL CAREER, IT'S NEVER LIKE THIS.

RATBERT THE CONSULTANT

...THEN WE'LL TURN OFF THE EXISTING COMPUTER SYSTEMS AND FIRE UP THE NEW ONE.

WHAT IF THE NEW SYSTEM DOESN'T WORK ON THE FIRST TRY? WON'T THE ECONOMIC IMPACT BE DEVASTATING?

LET ME CHECK MY CONTRACT...

NOPE. I GET PAID EXACTLY THE SAME.

YEAH, SAME HERE.

I AM ONLY AN INTERN, BUT MAY I MAKE A SUGGESTION?

THE ELBONIAN DATABASE SYSTEM YOU'RE INSTALLING FOR OUR COMPANY WILL NEVER WORK... UNLESS I REWRITE THE ENTIRE THING WITH JUST SIX KEYSTROKES...

DONE

I THOUGHT THIS WAS ONLY POSSIBLE IN BAD MOVIES.

HEY, LET'S HACK INTO NATO'S SYSTEM. I CAN GUESS THEIR PASSWORD IN THREE TRIES.

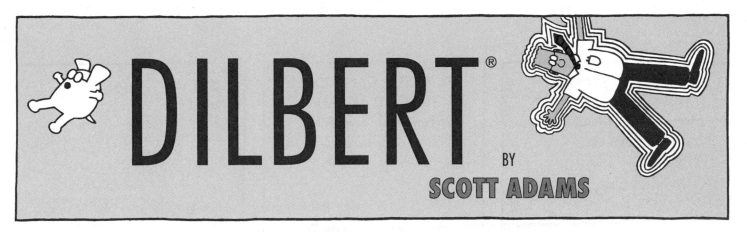

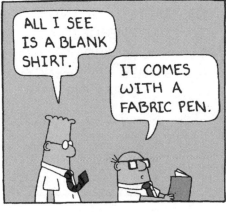

I'D LIKE A DIRECT FLIGHT... AISLE SEAT... AND AN UPGRADE TO FIRST CLASS IF POSSIBLE.

THE BEST I CAN DO IS TO PUT YOU IN AN OVERHEAD LUGGAGE BIN... WITH ONE STOP IN NORTH KOREA.

IS IT NON-SMOKING?

THAT DEPENDS ON HOW ACCURATE THE ANTI-AIRCRAFT FIRE IS.

THIS IS MARILYN VOS SAVANT, THE SMARTEST HUMAN ALIVE.

SHE WILL HELP YOU UNDERSTAND YOUR AIRLINE "OFTEN FLIER" PROGRAM.

I'M STUMPED.

AFTER THIS, COULD YOU TELL ME WHICH PHONE COMPANY SAVES ME THE MOST MONEY?

MY BRAIN'S TRYING TO ESCAPE; YOU SCARED IT.

THIS SUITCASE IS THE DECOY.

WHILE THE AIRLINE IS DISTRACTED TRYING TO LOSE THE DECOY, I'LL SNEAK ABOARD WITH THIS EMERGENCY CARRY-ON BAG.

WHAT IF THEY TRY TO MAKE YOU EAT THEIR FOOD?

FAKE VOMIT. THEY'LL THINK I ALREADY ATE.

DILBERT
BY
SCOTT ADAMS

DOGBERT'S TECH SUPPORT

THIS IS DOGBERT. HOW MAY I ABUSE YOU?

I NEED TO MOVE MY CURSOR TO THE RIGHT BUT MY MOUSE IS AT THE EDGE OF THE MOUSEPAD.

HAVE YOU TRIED REBOOTING WITHOUT SAVING YOUR FILES?

YEAH, SEVERAL TIMES.

HAVE YOU TRIED MOVING YOUR DESK?

IT DIDN'T WORK.

YOU NEED MY $800 MOUSEPAD UPGRADE.

WHAT ACCOUNT DOES THIS GET CHARGED TO?

"IDIOT EXPENSE," JUST LIKE EVERYTHING ELSE.

THE BUSINESS TRAVELER

CATBERT: EVIL H.R. DIRECTOR

YOU NEED A MILLION DOLLARS BUT I ONLY HAVE AUTHORITY TO SIGN FOR UP TO TEN THOUSAND.

BREAK IT INTO A HUNDRED SEPARATE BUSINESS CASES.

THANK YOU FOR YOUR VALUE-ADDED MANAGEMENT SUPPORT.

IT WAS NOTHING.

PER YOUR INSTRUCTIONS, MY REQUEST FOR A MILLION DOLLARS HAS BEEN BROKEN INTO ONE HUNDRED BUSINESS CASES.

EACH ONE IS FOR TEN THOUSAND DOLLARS, WHICH IS YOUR EXACT LEVEL OF APPROVAL AUTHORITY.

I MEANT I CAN APPROVE ANYTHING UNDER TEN THOUSAND DOLLARS... SO IF YOU WOULDN'T MIND...

KILLING YOU? NO, I WOULDN'T MIND A BIT.

OUR NEW CORPORATE POLICY IS THAT ALL EMPLOYEES MUST USE THE PRODUCTS WE SELL.

AAARGH!!!!! WHAT HAVE WE DONE TO DESERVE THIS ??!!!

SO YOU'RE SAYING THAT MANY OF THESE POLICIES ARE NOT INTENDED TO BE PUNISHMENTS?

YOU GET USED TO IT AFTER YOU LOSE YOUR WILL TO LIVE.

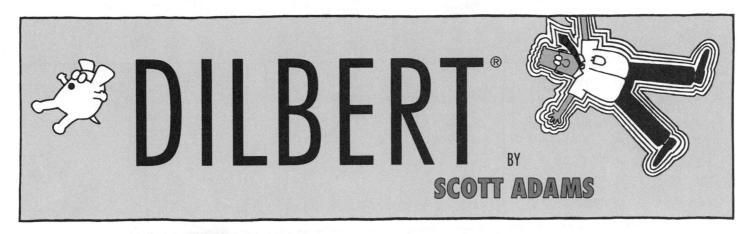

DILBERT

BY SCOTT ADAMS

BUYING A CAR

YOU'RE ONE TOUGH NEGOTIATOR.

THANKS.

IT ONLY TOOK YOU FOUR HOURS TO GET ME ALL THE WAY DOWN TO THE MANUFACTURER'S SUGGESTED RETAIL PRICE.

THERE'S NO PROFIT LEFT!! MY FAMILY WILL GO HUNGRY!! BWAA! BWAA!

SORRY.

I ASSUME YOU WANT THE RUST INHIBITOR COATING FOR ONLY $500.

UM... YEAH. RUST IS BAD.

YES!!

KA-CHING KA-CHING

SORRY

WE ALSO HAVE AN INVISIBLE SPRAY THAT PROTECTS AGAINST SCURVY AND TAX AUDITS.

WELL... OKAY.

INITIAL HERE IF YOU WANT YOUR AIRBAG TO BE FULL OF FRESH ASPEN AIR INSTEAD OF GRAVEL.

ONLY $600.

AND THE LEASE TERMS ARE ENGRAVED ON THIS FREE HOOD ORNAMENT!

BE GLAD THEY DIDN'T INSTALL IT.

YOU HAVE BEEN CHOSEN AS BILL GATES' TOWEL BOY. BUT FIRST YOU MUST ANSWER THIS QUIZ.

YOU'RE IN A ROOM WITH THREE MONKEYS. ONE HAS A BANANA, ONE HAS A STICK, ONE HAS NOTHING. WHICH PRIMATE IS THE SMARTEST?

UM...

I GUESS THE SUCCESSFUL TOWEL BOYS KNOW THAT HUMANS ARE PRIMATES TOO.

STUPID TRICK QUESTION.

HERE'S YOUR ANNUAL PERFORMANCE REVIEW, TINA.

I FOCUSED ON YOUR PERFORMANCE FOR THE PAST TWO WEEKS BECAUSE I DON'T REMEMBER ANYTHING FARTHER BACK.

I WAS ON VACATION FOR THE PAST TWO WEEKS !!!

NO TIME TO CHAT. I NEED TO SPREAD SOME MOTIVATION OVER HERE.

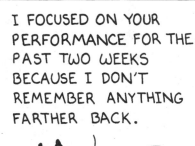

BUSINESSES USED TO BE LIKE CHRISTIANITY; IF YOU WERE FAITHFUL AND OBEDIENT, YOU COULD OBTAIN BLISS IN THE AFTERLIFE OF RETIRE-MENT.

NOW IT'S MORE OF A REINCARNATION MODEL. IF THE WORKER LEARNS ENOUGH IN HIS CURRENT JOB, HE CAN PROGRESS TO A HIGHER LEVEL OF EMPLOYMENT ELSEWHERE.

THESE ANALOGIES AREN'T WORKING FOR YOU, ARE THEY, BOB?

MY HOPE IS THAT ONE DAY I WILL BIO-DEGRADE AND BECOME "WD-40" OIL.

BAD NEWS ON YOUR PERFORMANCE REVIEW, WALLY.

EVERYONE PERFORMED THE SAME. BUT I'M REQUIRED TO RANK THE GROUP ON A BELL CURVE.

I HAD TO MAKE UP SOME FLAWS TO MOVE YOU DOWN THE CURVE. HERE'S A PEN. SIGN IT.

"EMPLOYEE DOES NOT WASH HANDS AFTER USING THE RESTROOM."

I CAN'T SIGN THIS PERFORMANCE REVIEW! IT'S FULL OF ALLEGED MISDEEDS THAT YOU INVENTED TO LOWER MY RATING!

YES, BUT I THINK IT REFLECTS THE SORT OF THINGS YOU MIGHT DO. I HAD TO MAKE ALL THE REVIEWS FIT A BELL CURVE.

I AM NOT SELLING CRACK FROM MY CUBICLE!!!

CATBERT: EVIL H.R. DIRECTOR

EFFECTIVE IMMEDIATELY, THE COMPANY WILL NO LONGER ALLOW TIME OFF FOR THE DEATH OF A FAMILY MEMBER.

THIS "FAMILY FRIENDLY" POLICY WILL REMOVE YOUR INCENTIVE TO EXTEND VACATIONS BY KILLING RELATIVES.

AND MORE GOOD NEWS: WE'RE CANCELING YOUR LIFE INSURANCE SO YOUR FAMILY WON'T TRY TO SNUFF YOU OUT EITHER.

DON'T MENTION ANY PROBLEMS WHEN YOU DO YOUR PRESENTATION TO SENIOR MANAGEMENT, ALICE.

THEY MIGHT TRY TO SOLVE THE PROBLEMS DURING THE MEETING. THAT WOULD BE A DISASTER.

AS FAR AS I CAN TELL, EVERY LAYER OF MANAGEMENT EXISTS FOR THE SOLE PURPOSE OF WARNING US ABOUT THE LAYER ABOVE.

ARE YOU SAYING THEY HAVE A PURPOSE?

I PUT YOU IN FOR A COMPLIMENT, ALICE.

IT'S NOT AUTOMATIC. THE APPLICATION MUST BE APPROVED BY THE EXECUTIVE REVIEW COMMITTEE.

EXECUTIVE REVIEW COMMITTEE

I DON'T THINK SO.

WE DON'T WANT THEM TO THINK COMPLIMENTS ARE AN ENTITLEMENT.

THE RESULTS OF THE EMPLOYEE SURVEY HAVE BEEN TABULATED.

AS ALWAYS, EMPLOYEES SAY THEY ARE UNDERPAID, BLAH, BLAH, BLAH, AND MANAGEMENT IS INCOMPETENT.

AND YOUR BIZARRE, UNWORLDLY RESPONSE WILL BE?

EVERYONE GETS A TRAVEL ALARM CLOCK WITH THE COMPANY LOGO!

CATBERT: EVIL H.R. DIRECTOR

WE'VE DECIDED TO LOWER YOUR BASE SALARY, WALLY.

I REALIZE THIS WILL BE A HARDSHIP. BUT IF YOU HAND ME YOUR NECKTIE I'LL SHOW YOU WHY THIS IS BEING DONE.

WHAT DID HE SAY WAS THE REASON?

"BECAUSE I CAN."

THE NETWORK WENT DOWN AND I LOST MY WORK.

THE SERVER CRASHED.

FROM NOW ON, I WANT ADVANCED NOTICE OF ANY UNPLANNED OUTAGES.

AND I NEED IT YESTERDAY.

I USED TO THINK THAT WAS JUST A FIGURE OF SPEECH.

AS YOU REQUESTED, HERE IS A SCHEDULE OF ALL FUTURE UNPLANNED NETWORK OUTAGES.

I TOOK THE INITIATIVE TO INCLUDE A SCHEDULE OF ALL FUTURE SICK DAYS, VOLCANIC ERUPTIONS, EARTH-QUAKES AND HURRICANES.

THIS IS THE POINT WHEN YOU REALIZE HOW STUPID YOUR REQUEST WAS AND WE HAVE A GOOD LAUGH.

DOES CNN KNOW ABOUT THIS?

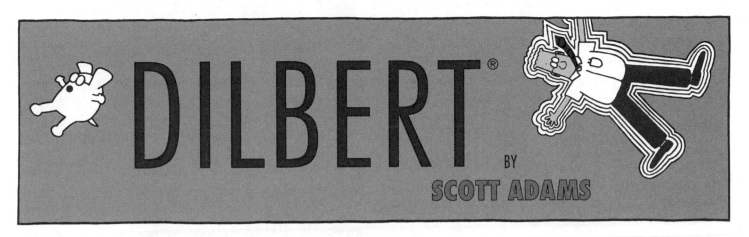

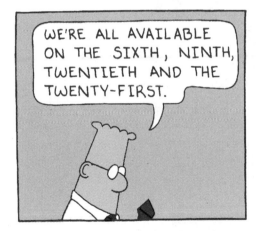

EVERY DEPARTMENT IS REQUIRED TO CREATE A WEB PAGE FOR OUR INTERNAL NETWORK.

IT SHOULD INCLUDE ENOUGH INFORMATION TO BE DIFFICULT TO MAINTAIN, BUT NOT SO MUCH THAT IT'S USEFUL.

AS A SECURITY PRECAUTION, WE'LL MAKE IT TOO DULL AND UNORGANIZED TO READ.

IS PORNOGRAPHY IN OR OUT?

I SPENT ALL WEEK TWEAKING HTML FOR MY INTRANET WEB PAGE. YOU SHOULD SEE IT, MOM.

I CONVERTED THE VIDEO OF MY BIRTH INTO AN MPEG FILE. ANYONE BEHIND THE FIRE WALL CAN VIEW IT.

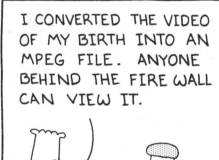

YOU SHOULD HEAR THE NICKNAME THEY HAVE FOR YOU AT WORK!

YOU SHOULD HEAR THE ONE I HAVE FOR YOU RIGHT NOW.

ALICE, I GAVE YOU A LOW PERFORMANCE RANKING BECAUSE YOU HAVEN'T BOTHERED ME ALL YEAR.

LOGICALLY, IF YOUR JOB WERE DIFFICULT AND IMPORTANT, YOU WOULD HAVE BROUGHT ME MANY ISSUES TO RESOLVE.

CAN YOU THINK OF **ANY** OTHER REASON I MIGHT NOT BRING YOU ISSUES?

YEAH, LAZINESS. BUT I GAVE YOU THE BENEFIT OF A DOUBT.

CATBERT: EVIL H.R. DIRECTOR

I WAS SO GOOD AT MY JOB THAT I NEVER NEEDED TO BOTHER MY BOSS. BUT HE GAVE ME A LOW RATING BECAUSE HE DIDN'T SEE ME STRUGGLING.

I MUST REFER TO MY HUMAN RESOURCES BINDERS TO SEE HOW TO DEAL WITH THIS.

DOWNSIZE DOWNSIZE HIRE LOSERS DOWNSIZE DOWNSIZE DOWNSIZE DOWNSIZE DOWNSIZE DOWNSIZE DOWNSIZE DOWNSIZE DOWNSIZE DOWNSIZE DOWNSIZE DOWNSIZE DOWNSIZE

© 1997 United Feature Syndicate, Inc.

2/6/97

DON'T MIND THE STOP-WATCH. I'M TESTING MY THEORY THAT PEOPLE GET DUMBER EVERY MINUTE.

IT'S NOT SO SIMPLE, DOGBERT. YOU ALSO HAVE TO CONSIDER MY "EMOTIONAL INTELLIGENCE," WHICH IS DEFINED IN A BOOK I HAVEN'T READ.

© 1997 United Feature Syndicate, Inc.

TWELVE SECONDS.

GIVE ME THAT WATCH, YOU HOG!

CLICK

2/7/97

MY OLD SLOGAN WAS, "WORK SMARTER NOT HARDER."

BUT PEOPLE KEPT LEAVING FOR COMPANIES THAT PAY MORE FOR LESS WORK.

© 1997 United Feature Syndicate, Inc.

WORK LIKE A FRIGHTENED IDIOT!

CATCHY.

2/8/97

I NEED A BULLET POINT FOR YOUR MONTHLY ACCOMPLISHMENTS, WALLY.

PUT ME DOWN FOR, "LEVERAGED SYNERGY ACROSS ALL TECHNOLOGY PLATFORMS."

THAT WAS YOUR ACCOMPLISHMENT LAST MONTH.

IT'S MORE OF A JOURNEY THAN A DESTINATION.

TODAY I'LL FIND OUT HOW BIG MY BONUS WILL BE.

AFTER ALL THE WORK I DID ON THAT PROJECT, I'M THINKING FOUR DIGITS, MAYBE FIVE.

LATER

HOW MANY DIGITS?

I USED ONE ON EACH HAND.

I NEED MY OWN SECRETARY. I'M TOO BUSY TO HELP YOU UNLESS I GET SOME SUPPORT.

TOO BUSY? YOU HAVEN'T DONE ANY WORK FOR ME IN SIX MONTHS.

OH, SUDDENLY THIS IS ABOUT YOU?

CAROL, DO YOU KNOW WHY MY RAISE HASN'T SHOWED UP IN MY PAY YET?

I HAVEN'T SUBMITTED THE PAPERWORK.

I'M TOO BUSY TO DO IT. MAYBE YOU SHOULD TALK TO MY BOSS ABOUT GETTING ME A SECRETARY.

CAROL, YOU ARE THE SECRETARY.

THAT'LL COST YOU ANOTHER MONTH.

MY RAISE DIDN'T GO THROUGH BECAUSE YOUR SECRETARY DIDN'T DO THE PAPERWORK.

I DEMAND THAT YOU INITIATE DISCIPLINARY ACTIONS AGAINST HER!

I'LL TRY, BUT...

CAROL, COULD YOU GET ME ONE OF THOSE DISCIPLINARY ACTION FORMS?

SURE, RIGHT AFTER MY SKI TRIP TO HELL.

THIS IS WENDY, MY NEW SECRETARY.

I DIDN'T KNOW SECRETARIES COULD HAVE SECRETARIES.

NOW WILL YOU HAVE TIME TO PROCESS MY PAY INCREASE? IT'S BEEN ON YOUR DESK FOR THREE MONTHS.

HA HA HA HA HA HA HA HA

HERE'S ANOTHER CASE WHERE MORE IS NOT BETTER.

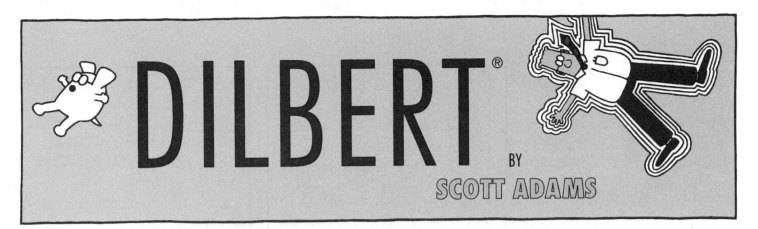

DILBERT

BY SCOTT ADAMS

YOU DIDN'T GIVE ME YOUR FIVE-YEAR BUDGET FORECAST.

YOU DIDN'T ASK FOR ONE.

IT WAS DISCUSSED AT THE PROJECT REVIEW MEETING.

YOU DIDN'T INVITE ME TO THAT MEETING.

DID YOU ACCOMPLISH ANYTHING THIS WEEK?

I TRAINED THE BATS WHO LIVE IN MY CUBICLE TO JUGGLE MUSHROOMS.

I'D LIKE TO START THE MEETING WITH A WHINY, UNANSWERABLE QUESTION.

WHY CAN'T ANYONE MAKE A DECISION AROUND HERE?!

THAT WAS GOOD.

MY LITTLE INTERN IS ALL GROWN UP.

SNIFF

HEY, THAT'S A UNION JOB. PUT IT DOWN OR I'LL FILE A GRIEVANCE.

I'M ONLY MOVING IT TEN FEET. IF I WAIT FOR A UNION PERSON, I'LL BE UNABLE TO DO MY JOB FOR A WEEK.

WATCH ME NOT CARE.

IF ANYONE SEES YOU MOVE THE PC TONIGHT, TRY SAYING YOU'RE JOHNNY CASH.

MAYBE I SHOULD JUST USE THE ELEVATOR.

THE BOLD COMMANDO STEALTHILY RELOCATES HIS PC AT NIGHT, THUS THWARTING BURDENSOME UNION RULES.

FREEZE, MISCREANT.

I HOPE THIS WORKS.

YOU DON'T LOOK LIKE JOHNNY CASH TO ME.

YOU'RE ACCUSED OF STEALING A COMPUTER. WE'LL REDUCE THE CHARGE TO "LEWD CONDUCT WITH APPLIANCES" IF YOU'LL PLEAD GUILTY.

THAT SOUNDS FAIR. PEOPLE WILL UNDERSTAND IT'S JUST A PLEA BARGAIN.

WOULD YOU LIKE A MINUTE ALONE WITH "MR. COFFEE"?

I'VE DECIDED TO ABANDON LOGIC AND MANAGE BY CLICHÉS.

IT WON'T BE EASY, BUT I'LL TAKE IT ONE BIRD AT A TIME.

AND REMEMBER, THE CUSTOMER IS ALWAYS RIGHT-HANDED.

THIS IS ACTUALLY AN IMPROVEMENT.

DILBERT

BY SCOTT ADAMS

I DREAD THIS PART OF THE STAFF MEETING.

LET'S GO AROUND THE TABLE AND DESCRIBE OUR ACCOMPLISHMENTS FOR THE WEEK.

WALLY?

IT WAS ANOTHER WEEK OF AMAZING SUCCESS IN WALLYVILLE.

ON MONDAY I REALIZED MY LEFT BUN HAD FALLEN ASLEEP.

I WAS SHOCKED. THE "BOYS" HAD ALWAYS WORKED AS A TEAM BEFORE.

THINKING QUICKLY, I SHIFTED MY WEIGHT TO MY RIGHT BUN AND HOPED FOR THE BEST.

THAT'S YOUR LEFT SIDE, NOT YOUR RIGHT.

THAT'S THE OTHER THING; APPARENTLY THE BOYS SWITCHED SIDES SOMETIME DURING THE NIGHT.

RATBERT, I'M GOING BACK INTO THE CONSULTING BUSINESS AND I NEED YOU TO BE MY ENGAGEMENT MANAGER.

YOU'LL SEEM VERY SMART IF YOU RANDOMLY COMBINE THE WORDS ON THIS LIST AND MAKE MANY REFERENCES TO "WAL-MART."

IT'S LIKE "WAL-MART." MIGRATE YOUR VALUE INTO THE WHITE SPACES OF THE ECOSYSTEM.

WOW! THAT'S ONE SMART RAT!

RATBERT THE CONSULTANT

"WAL-MART'S" BUSINESS STRATEGY WAS VERY SUCCESSFUL. YOU CAN LEARN FROM THEIR EXAMPLE.

DOES THEIR STRATEGY INVOLVE SITTING AROUND AND MAKING IRRELEVANT COMPARISONS TO OTHER COMPANIES?

ALL I KNOW FOR SURE IS THAT THEY DON'T LET RATS TRY ON ALL THE PANTYHOSE IN THE STORE.

GOOD STRATEGY.

RATBERT THE CONSULTANT

YOUR STRATEGY OPTIONS CAN BE SHOWN IN THIS MATRIX.

THE FOUR BOXES ARE "SOMETHING... SOMETHING... SOME OTHER THING AND WHATEVER."

IN PHASE TWO I HOPE TO TURN THIS MATRIX INTO CONCENTRIC CIRCLES WITH LABELS AND ARROWS.

I'M UNDER THE CONSULTANT'S SPELL.

RATBERT THE CONSULTANT

I AM UNDER YOUR CONSULTING SPELL.

REALLY?

YOUR OVERLY COMPLICATED MATRICES AND DIAGRAMS HAVE CONVINCED ME OF YOUR INTELLECTUAL SUPERIORITY.

I AM AFRAID TO ACT WITHOUT YOUR APPROVAL.

DID I SAY YOU COULD PUT YOUR ARMS UP LIKE THAT?

OUR BOSS HAS FALLEN UNDER THE SPELL OF A CONSULTANT.

MUST... MAKE ASSUMPTIONS.

MUST... WRITE... LARGE CHECKS TO CONSULTANT... BECAUSE... EMPLOYEES... ARE ... MORONS.

JUST BECAUSE WE PAY INEXPERIENCED STRANGERS TO TELL US HOW TO DO OUR JOBS, THAT DOESN'T MEAN WE'RE MORONS!

YEAH!

IT'S A COINCI-DENCE.

RATBERT THE CONSULTANT

NOW THAT YOU'RE UNDER MY SPELL, I'D LIKE TO SIT ON YOUR HEAD AND PLAY BULLDOZER.

MAKE SOME ENGINE NOISES WITH YOUR LIPS!

HA HA!!

BRBRBR BRBRBR

DO YOU THINK OUR CONSULTANT HAS TOO MUCH POWER?

NAH. HE'S BARELY MOVING THAT FILE CABINET.

BRBR BRBR BRBR

DILBERT

BY
SCOTT ADAMS

YOU'RE PROBABLY WONDERING HOW MY DAY WAS.

IT WAS TERRIBLE...

UNTIL I DID THIS!

IT ALL STARTED WHEN I DELUDED MYSELF INTO THINKING MY OPINIONS MATTERED.

I SPRANG INTO ACTION LIKE A CHEETAH ON A TRAMPOLINE!

I DREW LINES AND BOXES AND ARROWS FOR HOURS.

IT WAS PURE ADRENALINE.

SUDDENLY, TROUBLE STRUCK! IT WOULDN'T FIT ON ONE PAGE!!

SO I SHRUNK EVERYTHING UNTIL IT WAS TOTALLY UNREADABLE.

AND IT FIT!!

THE MORAL OF THE STORY IS THAT YOU DON'T HAVE TO FEEL BAD JUST BECAUSE YOU'RE TOTALLY WORTHLESS.

I'D MOCK YOU BUT THE CHALLENGE IS GONE.

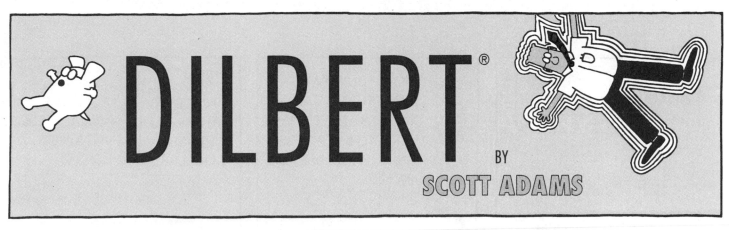

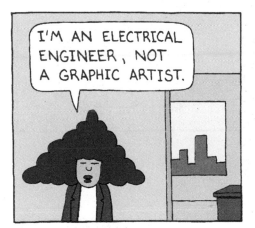

YOU ARE GUILTY OF BEING A TECHNICAL WRITER WITH AN UNNATURAL ATTRACTION TO AN ENGINEER.

IT'S NOT A MAJOR SIN, SO YOU ONLY GO TO HECK. I'M PHIL, THE PRINCE OF INSUFFICIENT LIGHT.

HECK

SIT DOWN AND TYPE, "I PROACTIVELY LEVERAGE MY SYNERGIES," A HUNDRED TIMES.

NO-O-O!!!

IT'S CALLED A "SMART CARD," AND WE SHOULD BUILD OUR NEXT PRODUCT TO HANDLE THIS SORT OF PAYMENT TECHNOLOGY.

AAAGH!!

FOOP

I'VE NEVER SEEN THAT HAPPEN.

HIS BODY REJECTED THE "SMART CARD."

I'VE INVENTED A QUANTUM COMPUTER, CAPABLE OF INTERACTING WITH MATTER FROM OTHER UNIVERSES TO SOLVE COMPLEX EQUATIONS.

ACCORDING TO CHAOS THEORY, YOUR TINY CHANGE TO ANOTHER UNIVERSE WILL SHIFT ITS DESTINY, POSSIBLY KILLING EVERY INHABITANT.

SHIFT HAPPENS.

FIRE IT UP.

I STUDIED YOUR TECHNICAL RECOMMENDATION AND DECIDED IT'S IMPOSSIBLE.

I ALREADY DID IT.

IT WILL NEVER WORK.

IT'S WORKING PERFECTLY.

YOU SPELLED THIS WORD WRONG.

THAT'S A NUMBER.

AVOID THE POINTY-HAIRED BOSS TODAY. I PROVED HIM WRONG ABOUT SOMETHING.

OH, TERRIFIC. NOW HE'S IN A STATE OF BOSS DISEQUILIBRIUM UNTIL HE PROVES HE'S RIGHT ABOUT SOMETHING.

THEY'RE **PHOTOCOPIES!** YOU DON'T NEED TO PROOFREAD **EACH ONE!**

WE'LL SEE ABOUT THAT.

WE PLAN TOO MUCH. FROM NOW ON WE'LL HAVE A BIAS FOR ACTION.

I WANT POSTERS THAT PROCLAIM OUR COMMITMENT TO ACTION. AND I WANT THEM SOON!

"MEASURE ONCE. CUT TWICE."

I LIKE IT.

TOLD YOU.

DILBERT®

BY SCOTT ADAMS

THIS SECURITY SYSTEM COST A FORTUNE BUT IT'S WORTH IT.

I PUT A CAMERA IN EVERY ROOM TO DETER ANY CRIMINAL ACTIVITY.

WE MAY NOW GO TO THE PARK KNOWING OUR FORTRESS IS PROTECTED.

I CAN'T WAIT TO SHOW MY KIDS WHAT I DO AT WORK.

I CAN ONLY THINK OF ONE THING WORSE THAN HAVING ALL OF MY STUFF STOLEN.

AND THAT IS HAVING SOME OF IT RETURNED.

THIS THING IS HIDEOUS IN GOOD LIGHT.

Editor's Note: On April Fool's Day, 1997, 46 syndicated cartoonists perpetrated a great hoax on newspaper comics readers by swapping strips for the day. One result was the above Dilbert strip. Scott Adams said of the swap-fest, "I think it was Nostradamus who predicted that when Pat Boone sings heavy metal and Bil Keane [Family Circus] draws Dilbert, it's a sign of the approaching apocalypse." (We say, "Duck!")

I HATE TO INTERRUPT YOUR LOUD CONVERSATION OUTSIDE MY CUBICLE...

BUT IF YOU DON'T GO AWAY, I'LL POUND YOUR INCONSIDERATE HEAD SO FAR INTO YOUR TORSO THAT YOU HAVE TO DROP YOUR PANTS TO SAY HELLO.

DID YOU JUST HEAR A STRANGE NOISE?

IT SOUNDED LIKE, "MELP! MELP!"

I'M SENDING YOU TO A TRAINING COURSE THAT RUNS AT NIGHT SO YOU WON'T MISS ANY WORK.

IT MIGHT SEEM LIKE AN IMMORAL ABUSE OF MY POWER, BUT I LIKE TO CALL IT "A MUTUAL INVESTMENT IN YOUR CAREER."

MUST... CONTROL... FIST... OF... DEATH...

AND THEY HAVE VENDING MACHINES IF YOU GET HUNGRY!

COMPANY TRAINING

LET'S GO AROUND THE ROOM AND WE'LL EACH SAY WHAT WE HOPE TO LEARN.

I HOPE TO LEARN WHETHER THAT THING ON YOUR HEAD IS A BAD TOUPEE, A DEAD ANIMAL, OR A HIDEOUS FREAK OF NATURE.

CAN I CALL THAT "GENERAL"?

S. Adams

© 1997 United Feature Syndicate, Inc.

4/3/97
4/1/97
4/5/97

DILBERT BY SCOTT ADAMS

DOGBERT PRESENTS

THE LIFE CYCLE OF A BUSINESS IDEA

THE BRAIN CREATES AN IDEA.

MMM

THE MOUTH — OPERATING INDEPENDENTLY OF THE BRAIN — CREATES WORDS.

LET'S FORM PROACTIVE SYNERGY RESTRUCTURING TEAMS.

THE WORDS ARE WRITTEN ON LARGE PAPER.

IDIOT.

Let's form synergy

THE LARGE PAPER IS DELIVERED TO A BITTER SECRETARY.

PLEASE?

GRRRR

THE SECRETARY TYPES IT.

"LET'S...FORM... PROTEIN... SYMPHONY REACTIONARY... TEENS."

CLOSE ENOUGH

THE TYPED NOTES ARE DELIVERED TO THE STAFF.

DROP IT IN THE "TO DO BASKET."

REPEAT.

MMM

ALICE, YOUR PERFORMANCE IS GOOD, BUT YOU MUST LEARN TO DEAL WITH AMBIGUITY.

DID I JUST GET BLAMED FOR YOUR INDECISIVE LEADERSHIP?

I'M NOT INDECISIVE; I'M FLEXIBLE.

THAT WOULD EXPLAIN HOW YOUR HEAD GOT WHERE IT IS.

HERE'S THE NEW ORG CHART. I HAD TO REARRANGE THE LAYOUT TO MAKE IT FIT.

WHY IS MY BOX LOWER THAN ALICE AND WALLY'S?

IT MEANS NOTHING... NOTHING AT ALL.

OKAY, WHO TOLD YOU THAT EVERY YEAR I FISH YOUR SECRETARIES' DAY CARD OUT OF YOUR TRASH AND SAVE IT FOR NEXT TIME?

WHAT?

THE NEW ORG CHART HAS MY NAME LOWER THAN YOURS, BUT IT DOESN'T MEAN ANYTHING.

SEE? IT WOULDN'T ALL FIT ACROSS THE PAGE. IT'S JUST A GRAPHICAL LAYOUT THING, THAT'S ALL.

HEY, DIL-BOY, PUT A HEAD ON THIS AND FETCH MY MAIL.

ARE YOU ASKING ME TO BE YOUR MENTOR?

I NOTICE THAT THE NEW ORG CHART HAS YOUR BOX LOWER THAN BEFORE.

IT MEANS NOTHING.

PERHAPS. BUT YOUR BOX SEEMS SMALLISH. AND YOUR REPORTING LINE BRUSHES AGAINST MY BOX.

IT MEANS NOTHING.

NO, I'M SURE THIS MEANS I'M YOUR NEW BOSS.

I WONDER IF I KILLED SOMEONE IN A PREVIOUS LIFE.

I DON'T CARE WHAT IT "LOOKS" LIKE ON THE ORG CHART! YOU'RE AN INTERN, NOT MY BOSS!

I JUST SAW THE NEW ORG CHART. CONGRATULATIONS ON YOUR PROMOTION, ASOK!

LET'S GO MAKE SOME STRATEGIES AND PRETEND IT'S WORK!

NOT SO LOUD. THE L-U-S-E-R MIGHT HEAR.

Bonk Bonk

CAROL, I DON'T MEAN TO BE CRITICAL ABOUT THE DEPARTMENT PHONE LIST YOU PUT TOGETHER...

BUT IT'S TRADITIONAL TO LIST PEOPLE ALPHABETICALLY, NOT SORTED BY PHONE NUMBER.

BECAUSE WHAT POSSIBLE USE...?

INCOMING CALL FROM... LET'S SEE... IT'S WALLY... I CAN IGNORE IT.

Ring

DILBERT

BY **SCOTT ADAMS**

HERE'S MY PROJECT PLAN AS YOU REQUESTED.

OUR TEAM IS ALREADY WORKING DAY AND NIGHT ON OTHER PROJECTS.

I ASSUMED WE'D GIVE UP EATING, SLEEPING AND BATHING TO FIT THIS IN.

BY THE SECOND WEEK WE'LL BE STARVING, DELIRIOUS AND STINKING.

WE'LL BE LIKE WILD, UNPREDICTABLE ANIMALS.

SPECIFICALLY, WE'D BE LIKE WILD CHIPMUNKS. NONE OF US ARE VERY AGGRESSIVE.

THIS CLIP-ART REPRESENTS US IN WEEK THREE AS A PILE OF DEAD CHIPMUNKS.

NOW HE WANTS IT IN TWO WEEKS?

NEVER MIX SARCASM WITH GOOD CLIP-ART.

ALICE, I NEED THIS ASAP.

ASAP? DOES THAT STAND FOR <u>A</u> <u>S</u>TUPID-<u>A</u>CTING <u>P</u>ERSON, I.E., SOMEONE WHO IGNORES TASKS UNTIL THE DEADLINE?

THAT WAS EMBARRASSING. I HOPE THE OTHER THINGS I SAY DON'T MEAN ANYTHING.

CATBERT: EVIL H.R. DIRECTOR

THE COMPANY HAS TAKEN OUT A LIFE INSURANCE POLICY ON YOU, WALLY.

WE PAY THE PREMIUMS AND WE COLLECT THE INSURANCE WHEN YOU DIE.

IS THIS BECAUSE I'M SO VALUABLE TO THE COMPANY?

IT'S BECAUSE WE THINK YOU'LL BE MORE VALUABLE DEAD.

THIS IS EXACTLY WHY I DON'T LIKE CATS.

THERE'S BEEN A LOT OF JOKING AND GRUMBLING SINCE THE COMPANY TOOK OUT LIFE INSURANCE POLICIES ON ALL OF YOU.

SO WE'RE HAVING THESE CATERED LUNCH MEETINGS TO DISCUSS YOUR FEELINGS.

DO YOU WANT THE MAD COW BURGER OR THE CHICKEN BONE SURPRISE?

I FOUND ANOTHER DEAD EMPLOYEE IN THE CONFERENCE ROOM.

I DON'T KNOW WHAT GOT HIM — THE BOREDOM OR THE HARD WORK. BUT HEADCOUNT IS DOWN ONE AND THE COMPANY HAS LIFE INSURANCE ON HIM!

IT LOOKS LIKE I FOUND MY "EMPLOYEE OF THE WEEK."

CATBERT: EVIL H.R. DIRECTOR

WALLY, THE COMPANY BOUGHT A LIFE INSURANCE POLICY ON YOU.

OUR PLAN IS TO RAISE YOUR BLOOD PRESSURE TO DANGEROUS LEVELS.

DID YOU KNOW THAT OUR CEO MAKES FIFTY TIMES YOUR SALARY EVEN THOUGH OUR STOCK IS DOWN?

OW! OW! OW!

YOUR SUCCESS AT WORK DEPENDS ON WHAT YOU HAVE IN YOUR HANDS WHEN YOU WALK AROUND.

A COFFEE CUP IS BAD. A DOCUMENT IS GOOD. A CIGARETTE IS BAD. A BINDER IS GOOD. BUT THE VERY WORST THING...

IT DOESN'T LOOK LIKE YOU'RE HEADING FOR THE FAST TRACK, WALLY.

ACTUALLY, I AM, UNLESS IT'S OCCUPIED.

MY STUDY SHOWS THAT THE COMPANIES WITH "FAMILY FRIENDLY" POLICIES HAVE HIGHER PROFITS.

QUESTION: DO FAMILY POLICIES CAUSE HIGH PROFITS OR DO HIGH PROFITS SIMPLY CAMOUFLAGE THE TRUE COSTS OF THE POLICIES?

WE'LL TAKE A FIVE-MINUTE BREAK SO THE MARRIED PEOPLE CAN SLAP YOU FOR ASKING THAT.

OUCH!

THIS SO-CALLED "FAMILY FRIENDLY" POLICY IS LIKE A TAX ON CHILDLESS PEOPLE.

YOU GET CHILD-CARE; I GET LOWER PROFIT-SHARING. YOU GET TIME OFF FOR FAMILY; I GET TO PICK UP YOUR SLACK ...

I'M A VICTIM, BUT IN SOME STRANGE WAY I'M ENJOYING IT.

THEN YOU'LL LOVE THIS.

I'M GOING HOME EARLY BECAUSE MY KID IS SICK.

REMEMBER, WE HAVE A NEW "FAMILY FRIENDLY" POLICY.

WE DO?

IS THAT WHY MY FAMILY SEEMS SO FRIENDLY?

MAYBE, BUT I'D TEST 'EM FOR DRUGS.

CATBERT: EVIL H.R. DIRECTOR

I'M BEING DISCRIMINATED AGAINST BECAUSE I TAKE TIME OFF FOR FAMILY EMERGENCIES.

I'LL HANDLE THIS BY TELLING YOUR BOSS THAT YOU RATTED HIM OUT TO THE DIRECTOR OF HUMAN RESOURCES.

I THOUGHT WE HAD A "FAMILY FRIENDLY" POLICY.

THE KEY WORD IS <u>FRIENDLY</u>. YOU'VE BEEN ACTING AS IF YOU <u>LOVE</u> YOUR FAMILY.

GOOD NEWS! OUR BUSINESS PLAN IS IN COMPLETE DISARRAY!

FREE TIME!! NO DELIVERABLES!!! AND IT'S NOT <u>OUR</u> FAULT!

YIPPEE!!

DO YOU REALIZE THAT ALL OUR JOY COMES FROM PERVERSE SOURCES?

I DIDN'T KNOW THERE WAS AN ALTERNATIVE.

ALICE, OUR BUSINESS PLAN IS IN COMPLETE DISARRAY SO WE'RE TAKING A THREE-HOUR LUNCH. WANT TO JOIN US?

NO, I'VE GOT TO WORK HARDER THAN EVER TO TURN THIS SITUATION AROUND!

SOMETIMES IT'S HARD TO DISTINGUISH BETWEEN DEDICATION AND INSANITY.

WHICH ONE ARE WE?

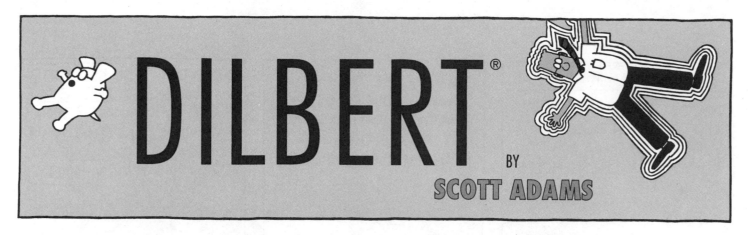

DILBERT®

BY SCOTT ADAMS

WHO WAS THE WORLD'S FIRST SALESPERSON, DOGBERT?

SOME PEOPLE SAY IT WAS A GUY NAMED NOAH.

NOAH'S LAST NAME WAS CONTENT.

I HAVE A BIG, CURLY STICK AND I DON'T EVEN KNOW WHY.

HIS JOB WAS TO SELL AN ARK CRUISE TO ANIMALS.

DID I SAY ARK? I MEANT YACHT.

HE INVENTED SOMETHING CALLED SALES-BABBLE TO DISGUISE HIS MOTIVES.

WE'LL PARTNER TO LEVERAGE OUR VALUE-ADDS IN A WIN-WIN PROPOSITION.

HE PIONEERED THE LAME JOKE.

HOW'S THE WEATHER UP THERE? HEE HEE!

WHEN HE COULDN'T REACH QUOTA, HE GOT CREATIVE.

STRAP THIS TO YOUR HEAD AND DON'T ASK QUESTIONS.

BUT HIS GREATEST INNOVATION HE CALLED "BLAMING ENGINEERING."

I CAN'T FIND THE HONEY SPA.

THINK FAST.

I CALCULATED THE TOTAL TIME THAT HUMANS HAVE WAITED FOR WEB PAGES TO LOAD...

IT CANCELS OUT ALL THE PRODUCTIVITY GAINS OF THE INFORMATION AGE.

SOMETIMES I THINK THE WEB IS A BIG PLOT TO KEEP PEOPLE LIKE ME AWAY FROM NORMAL SOCIETY.

UH-OH, HE'S ON TO ME.

ARE YOU TELLING ME THAT YOU INVENTED THE FIRST WEB BROWSER?

NOT ALONE. I WORKED WITH OUR GARBAGE MAN.

FLASHBACK

I WONDER HOW LONG PEOPLE WOULD SIT IN FRONT OF A COMPUTER WAITING FOR NOTHING.

LET'S FIND OUT!

WHAT IF THIS THING GETS OUT OF HAND?

WE'LL BLAME IT ON SOME DRUNKEN COLLEGE KID.

FLASHBACK TO THE INVENTION OF THE FIRST WEB BROWSER

WHAT SHOULD WE CALL OUR PRANK, DOGBERT?

WELL, IT'S DESIGNED TO MAKE MILLIONS OF PEOPLE SIT AROUND WAITING FOR NOTHING TO HAPPEN...

A FEW YEARS LATER

HEY, I CAN ALMOST SEE A RECOGNIZABLE BLOTCH! THIS IS AWESOME!

NOTE

FLASHBACK: DOGBERT AND THE WORLD'S SMARTEST GARBAGEMAN INVENT THE FIRST WEB BROWSER AS A PRACTICAL JOKE.

IT'S OUT OF CONTROL.

I WONDER WHAT WILL HAPPEN TO THAT COLLEGE KID WE FRAMED

HE'LL BE OKAY.

WHERE WOULD YOU LIKE THIS BUSHEL OF MONEY?

STACK IT NEXT TO THE PHOTOGRAPHERS.

© 1997 United Feature Syndicate, Inc.
5/8/97

WALLY, WE DON'T HAVE TIME TO GATHER THE PRODUCT REQUIREMENTS AHEAD OF TIME.

I WANT YOU TO START DESIGNING THE PRODUCT ANYWAY. OTHERWISE IT WILL LOOK LIKE WE AREN'T ACCOMPLISHING ANYTHING.

OF ALL MY PROJECTS, I LIKE THE DOOMED ONES BEST.

NEWS

© 1997 United Feature Syndicate, Inc.
5/9/97

WE DID AN INDUSTRY SURVEY TO SEE HOW YOUR SALARIES COMPARED TO THE AVERAGE.

WE DIDN'T GET THE NUMBERS WE HOPED FOR, SO WE BROADENED THE DEFINITION OF "OUR INDUSTRY."

I'M SO HAPPY TO BE IN THE INDUSTRY OF "HIGH TECHNOLOGY, TEXTILE WORKERS, TEEN-AGERS, AND DEAD PEOPLE."

I FEEL OVERPAID.

© 1997 United Feature Syndicate, Inc.
5/10/97

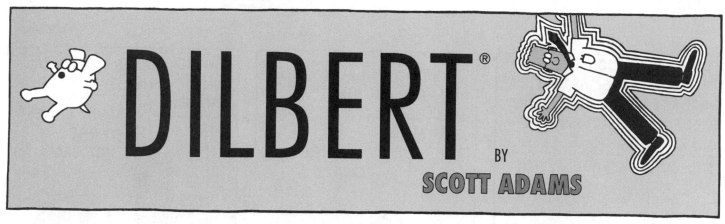

DILBERT®

BY **SCOTT ADAMS**

I AM CARL, THE CUBICLE DWELLERS' FRIEND.

I TRAVEL FROM CUBICLE TO CUBICLE TO TELL PEOPLE HOW HARD I'M WORKING.

I AM WORKING SO-O-O-O HARD. WORK, WORK, WORK. IT'S ALL I DO.

HOW IS THAT POSSIBLE?

YOU WALK AROUND ALL DAY WITH THAT COFFEE CUP RESTING ON YOUR BELLY.

DOES YOUR JOB DESCRIPTION SAY "TRANSPORT COFFEE CUP ON BELLY"?

HE'S A TERRIBLE CONVERSATIONALIST.

HOW MANY MILES PER GALLON DO YOU GET?

HYPOTHETICALLY, IF YOU WERE DOWNSIZED, HOW WOULD THE CUP GET AROUND?

WHAT'S WRONG WITH THESE PEOPLE?

119

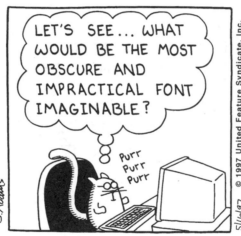

DILBERT

BY
SCOTT ADAMS

THANK YOU. PLEASE COME AGAIN.

AFTER I'M DEAD.

IF WE EACH PUT IN TWELVE DOLLARS, THAT WILL GIVE HER A HEALTHY FOURTEEN PERCENT TIP.

THE SERVICE WAS EXCELLENT. I'LL PUT IN A LITTLE EXTRA.

ME TOO.

ME TOO.

THAT GIVES US...UM... ONLY THIRTY-FOUR DOLLARS.

ONE OF US IS A CHEAP, LYING, UNSCRUPULOUS WEASEL.

OR MAYBE THE SERVICE WAS BAD.

SHE DIDN'T SMILE ENOUGH.

SAME AS LAST WEEK.

WALLY, TWO THINGS...

NUMBER ONE, I WANT YOU TO CHAIR THE "FUN COMMITTEE" TO IMPROVE EMPLOYEE MORALE.

TWO, ACCORDING TO THIS REPORT, YOU'VE BEEN USING THE INTERNET FOR PERSONAL REASONS.

I WAS TRYING TO DECIDE IF YOU'RE STUPID OR JUST VERY IGNORANT.

THEN I THOUGHT, "WHOA, DOGBERT, YOU'RE BEING NARROW-MINDED ABOUT THIS."

YOU COULD EASILY BE BOTH.

IT ONLY LOOKS EASY.

IT IS PHYSICALLY IMPOSSIBLE FOR ME TO FINISH BOTH OF MY PROJECTS ON TIME. WHICH ONE IS MORE IMPORTANT?

HMM... IF I ABSOLUTELY HAD TO CHOOSE BETWEEN THEM, I'D SAY...

DO THEM BOTH ON TIME.

WOW. WHEN YOU DO THAT WITH YOUR ARMS, IT CREATES THE ILLUSION THAT YOU'RE THINKING.

WHAT YOU NEED IS A THIRD PROJECT.

ANY EMPLOYEE WHO USES THE INTERNET FOR NON-BUSINESS PURPOSES WILL BE FIRED.

AND ANY EMPLOYEE WHO SITS IN A COMPANY CHAIR WHILE HAVING A PERSONAL THOUGHT WILL BE EXECUTED BY SECURITY.

THE GREAT THING ABOUT SENSELESS, SADISTIC POLICIES IS THAT THEY DON'T REQUIRE A LOT OF EXPLANATION.

I WROTE THIS LABOR-SAVING SOFTWARE. WATCH IT DO ITS THING.

HOW CAN YOU TELL IF IT'S WORKING?

YOU DON'T SEE ANY LABOR HAPPENING AROUND HERE, DO YOU?

I'VE DECIDED TO BECOME A CONSULTANT IN THE FIELD OF OBVIOUS GENERALITIES.

I'LL WORK FOR SMALL BUSINESSES THAT ARE RUN BY ARTISTS. THEY'LL THINK I'M BRILLIANT, WHICH I AM.

WHOA! ARE YOU SAYING WE NEED REVENUE TO MAKE PROFIT ??

OUCH! I'VE GOT A HEADACHE ON ONE SIDE.

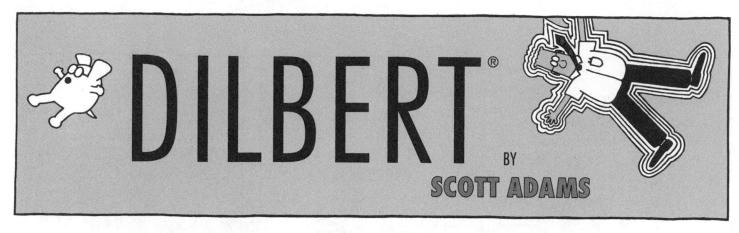

LATELY I'VE BEEN FEELING DISCOURAGED ABOUT MY JOB.

YOU SHOULD TALK TO OUR POINTY-HAIRED BOSS.

THAT'LL CHEER YOU UP.

MAYBE YOU'RE RIGHT. ALL I NEED IS A LITTLE PEP TALK FROM OUR LEADER.

HA HA HA! HEE HEE!

YOU THINK YOU'RE DISCOURAGED...

I'VE BEEN STUCK IN THIS DEAD-END JOB FOR YEARS, GRINDING AWAY, DAY AFTER DAY.

AND ALL I HAVE TO SHOW FOR IT IS HIGH BLOOD PRESSURE AND WORTHLESS STOCK OPTIONS.

IT'S SO GRATIFYING TO WATCH THEM GROW UP.

I NEED THE NUMBER FOR DOCTOR KEVORKIAN.

I HAVE A CLOUD OF DOOM THAT ZAPS EVERYONE NEAR ME ONCE A MINUTE.

DOOM

I'M LOOKING FOR A WOMAN WHO DOESN'T THINK THAT PAST BEHAVIOR IS AN INDICATION OF THE FUTURE.

DOOM

ZAP!

...A WOMAN WITH ABSOLUTELY NO SENSE OF PATTERN RECOGNITION.

DOOM

OUCH. I'M GLAD THAT WON'T HAPPEN AGAIN.

THE ONLY WAY TO GET RID OF YOUR CLOUD OF DOOM IS TO TRANSFER IT TO A NEW HOST BODY.

DOOM

I WILL ACCOMPLISH THIS WITH THE HELP OF YOUR POINTY-HAIRED BOSS AND A CLUELESS CO-WORKER NAMED TIM.

WE'RE SECURE. BEGIN TRANSFER.

TIM, YOUR NEW JOB WILL BE DIRECTOR OF SPECIAL PROJECTS.

DOOM

ALICE, I UNDERSTAND YOU HAD A CONVERSATION WITH MY BOSS WITHOUT MY APPROVAL.

WE DON'T WANT TO GIVE MIXED MESSAGES. IT WOULD BE VERY BAD IF SHE GOT ANY MIXED MESSAGES.

I JUST GAVE HER AN HONEST STATUS REPORT.

AAARGH!!! MIXED MESSAGES!

DILBERT
BY
SCOTT ADAMS

I FORGOT MY UMBRELLA. I'M SOAKED.

WHY DON'T YOU TOSS YOUR CLOTHES IN THE MICROWAVE AND DRY THEM OFF?

WOULD THAT WORK?

SIXTY MINUTES OUGHT TO DO IT.

WE'LL GUARD THE DOOR TO THE BREAK ROOM.

YOU KNOW, EVER SINCE THE DOWNSIZING BEGAN, I'VE FELT MUCH LESS COMPANY LOYALTY.

ME TOO.

WHY ARE YOU TWO SO HAPPY?

THERE ARE FREE GOODIES IN THE BREAK ROOM.

I PUT TOGETHER SOME GUIDING PRINCIPLES FOR OUR NETWORK ARCHITECTURE.

I SURE HOPE THIS ISN'T A BUNCH OF OBVIOUS IDEAS DISGUISED WITH TECHNO-JARGON AND UNCLEAR WRITING.

LET THE GAMES BEGIN.

SO TELL ME, DO SUSPENDERS CAUSE MUDDLED THINKING, OR IS IT THE OTHER WAY AROUND?

I'M GOING INTO BUSINESS AS A PROFESSIONAL BEARER OF BAD NEWS.

I'LL TRY TO FIND THE HUMOR THAT IS INHERENT IN EVERY TRAGIC SITUATION.

I GIVE UP. WHAT IS THE DIFFERENCE BETWEEN MY HUSBAND AND THE SEVENTIES POP GROUP "VILLAGE PEOPLE"?

THEY'RE COMING BACK.

DOGBERT: PROFESSIONAL BEARER OF BAD NEWS

WE CANNOT OFFER YOU A POSITION AT THIS TIME, BUT YOU ARE OBVIOUSLY QUALIFIED.

UNFORTUNATELY, THE OTHER SIX BILLION PEOPLE ON EARTH ARE MORE QUALIFIED.

WE'LL KEEP YOUR RÉSUMÉ ON FILE.

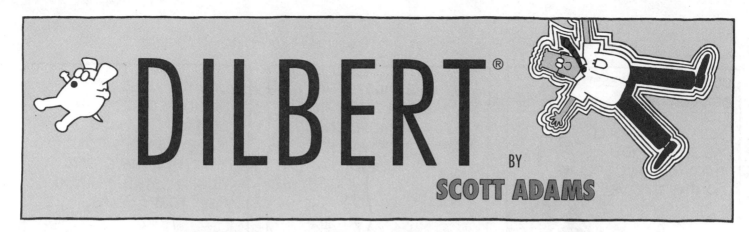

DILBERT

BY **SCOTT ADAMS**

I'M HAPPY TO AWARD THE "CLEAN CUBICLE AWARD" TO MATTHEW.

IT'S A TEN-DOLLAR "TRAVELERS CHECK."

WHERE'S MATTHEW?

HE WAS CRUELLY DOWNSIZED LAST MONTH.

HIS CUBICLE WAS CLEAN BECAUSE HE SHREDDED HIS IMPORTANT DOCUMENTS OUT OF SPITE.

ALL OF HIS FURNITURE AND EQUIPMENT WERE SCAVENGED BY BITTER EMPLOYEES WHO HAVE TO DO HIS WORK NOW.

THIS IS NOT HAVING THE MOTIVATIONAL IMPACT I HAD HOPED FOR.

6/8/57 — Dogbert's Birthday

OKAY... THE "TRAVELERS CHECK" WILL GO TO WHOEVER KNOWS WHAT NUMBER I'M THINKING.

THEY SURE WERE SORE LOSERS.

VISITING THE CUSTOMER

I BROUGHT DILBERT TO EXPLAIN WHAT MAKES OUR PRODUCT SPECIAL.

IT'S EXACTLY LIKE OUR COMPETITOR'S PRODUCT EXCEPT WE CHARGE MORE TO COVER THE COST OF OUR DECEPTIVE ADVERTISING.

WHILE YOU'RE UP, COULD YOU GET ME A CUP OF COFFEE?

VISITING THE CUSTOMER

NO ONE HAS EVER BEEN FIRED FOR BUYING OUR PRODUCT!

THAT'S TRUE.

THERE IS THE OCCASIONAL SAVAGE BEATING... AND MORE THAN OUR SHARE OF SUICIDES...

BUT THAT HAS "STATISTICAL CLUSTERING" WRITTEN ALL OVER IT.

SOMEDAY IT WILL BE POSSIBLE TO CLONE OUR BOSS.

BUT THE CLONE WOULD HAVE NO EXPERIENCE AND NO KNOWLEDGE.

I JUST SENT AN E-MAIL MESSAGE TO JAPAN. I DON'T KNOW THE LANGUAGE SO I TOOK YOUR ADVICE AND TYPED IT ALL IN CAPS.

WOW. THAT PUT IT ALL IN PERSPECTIVE.

DILBERT

BY
SCOTT ADAMS

ASOK THE INTERN EXPLAINS THE NEW RULES OF BODY LANGUAGE

FAKE HAPPINESS

THIS MEANS: I AM NOT MOTIVATED BY THE SIZE OF MY PAYCHECK.

AHH!! WAHH! WAHH!

THIS MEANS: I AM SLIGHTLY CONCERNED ABOUT THE IMPENDING REORGANIZATION.

THIS MEANS: I HAVE DECIDED TO WORK IN THE MARKETING FIELD.

COUNTER-CLOCKWISE SPIN

THIS MEANS: I AM BEING SARCASTIC.

OH, THERE'S A GOOD PLAN.

NOTE LIPS

THIS MEANS: THE RECENT EMPLOYEE SATISFACTION SURVEY HAS NOT CAPTURED THE EXTENT OF MY FEELINGS.

THIS MEANS: I THINK YOU ARE ATTRACTIVE BUT IT WOULD BE VERY UNPROFESSIONAL TO SHOW IT.

THIS MEANS: MY LOTTERY INVESTMENT PAID OFF.

YANK!

I SCHEDULED A TWO-HOUR T.H.N.P.L. MEETING FOR SEVEN O'CLOCK ON FRIDAY NIGHT.

T.H.N.P.L. STANDS FOR "TINA HAS NO PERSONAL LIFE." I'M SCHEDULING USELESS MEETINGS TO FILL THE VOID IN MY LIFE.

TINA, THIS IS INSANE.

ARE YOU SUGGESTING WE HAVE A MEETING TO DISCUSS IT? IS SATURDAY OKAY?

YOU'RE INVITED TO A FOUR-HOUR MEETING, ASOK.

TINA, IT WOULD SEEM THAT ALL OF YOUR MEETINGS HAVE NO PURPOSE OTHER THAN TO PROVIDE YOU WITH A SURROGATE SOCIAL LIFE.

CAN YOU BRING CHIPS?

I WISH, I WISH, I WISH I HAD A SPINE.

CATBERT: EVIL H.R. DIRECTOR

PEOPLE ARE COMPLAINING THAT YOU SCHEDULE UNNECESSARY MEETINGS AS A SUBSTITUTE FOR A FAMILY.

THAT'S RIDICULOUS! COME TO MY NEXT MEETING AND SEE FOR YOURSELF.

OKAY, I WILL.

I GOT US A FAMILY CAT. HOW WAS YOUR DAY, DEAR?

SOB

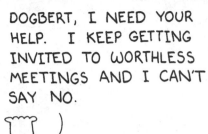

DOGBERT, I NEED YOUR HELP. I KEEP GETTING INVITED TO WORTHLESS MEETINGS AND I CAN'T SAY NO.

YOU CAN SAY NO TO ANYTHING. YOU HAVE SUCH A CLEARLY DEFINED SENSE OF SELF-INTEREST.

WILL YOU TEACH ME TO BE LIKE YOU?

NOPE... CAN'T BE BOTHERED.

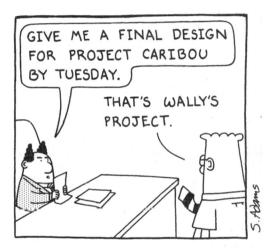

GIVE ME A FINAL DESIGN FOR PROJECT CARIBOU BY TUESDAY.

THAT'S WALLY'S PROJECT.

I KNOW, BUT I'M THINKING ABOUT IT NOW AND WALLY ISN'T IN THE ROOM.

TELL WALLY IT'S YOUR PROJECT NOW.

DO YOU SEE THIS THIMBLE? I KEEP MY MORALE IN IT.

... SO OUR POINTY-HAIRED BOSS PUT ME IN CHARGE OF YOUR PROJECT...

... BECAUSE I WAS STANDING IN HIS OFFICE WHEN HE THOUGHT ABOUT THE PROJECT.

IF IT MAKES YOU FEEL BETTER, YOU CAN KEEP YOUR MORALE IN THIS THIMBLE WITH MINE.

I KEEP MINE IN A "TIC TAC" CONTAINER WITH MY EGO.

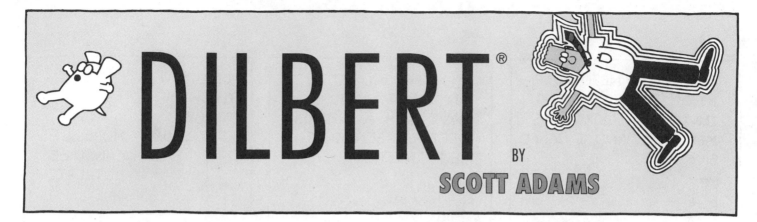

DILBERT

BY SCOTT ADAMS

I HAVE A GREAT IDEA TO SAVE MONEY.

WE CAN MAKE THE PHOTOCOPIER INK LAST LONGER BY ADDING WATER TO IT.

WOULDN'T THAT MAKE THE COPIES TOO LIGHT?

ORDINARILY, YES. BUT WE CAN COMPENSATE BY SETTING THE COPIER TO "DARKEN."

YOU'LL NEED SOMEONE TO IMPLEMENT THIS IDEA ... LET'S SEE.

HEY, HOW ABOUT DILBERT? HE ISN'T DOING MUCH WORK LATELY.

I'D DO IT MYSELF BUT THERE'S NO REASON TO WASTE A CREATIVE THINKER ON AN IMPLEMENTATION TASK.

ARE YOU STILL MAD THAT I GOT A BIGGER RAISE THAN YOU DID?

NO, I FOUND A CREATIVE WAY TO DEAL WITH IT.

CATBERT: EVIL H.R. DIRECTOR

NEW POLICY: KEY EMPLOYEES MUST TRAVEL ON SEPARATE FLIGHTS TO REDUCE RISK.

OTHER EMPLOYEES, SUCH AS WALLY, ARE ENCOURAGED TO TAKE UP DANGEROUS HOBBIES.

I'VE NOTICED THAT WHEN A NEW POLICY MENTIONS ME BY NAME, IT'S NEVER A GOOD THING.

ALICE, HERE'S A BONUS FOR YOUR GOOD WORK.

ON WHAT?

I CAN'T BE SPECIFIC, BECAUSE THEN YOU MIGHT DO IT AGAIN AND EXPECT ANOTHER BONUS.

CONGRATULATIONS; YOU'VE MOTIVATED ME TO ACT RANDOMLY.

I'M GOING OVER HERE AND I DON'T KNOW WHY.

I DID LESS WORK THAN USUAL THIS QUARTER AND I GOT A BONUS.

THE IMPLICATIONS ARE STAGGERING. THE ENTIRE SYSTEM OF CAPITALISM HAS A FLAWED PREMISE.

THERE'S ONLY ONE THING THAT COULD MAKE THIS BONUS MORE FRIGHTENING.

I GOT ONE, TOO.

I'M WRITING A BOOK THAT DEBUNKS THE EFFECTIVENESS OF BUSINESS CONSULTANTS.

BUT COMMON SENSE WOULD SAY THAT YOU'RE BEING A CONSULTANT YOURSELF, SO YOUR OPINION IS LOGICALLY FLAWED.

ONLY PEOPLE WITH NO COMMON SENSE WILL BUY YOUR BOOK.

I PREFER TO CALL THEM THE MASS MARKET.

FROM NOW ON, WE'LL NURTURE THE PASSION OF OUR REBELLIOUS EMPLOYEES AND FORM STRATEGIES AROUND THEM.

WE DON'T HAVE ANY REBELLIOUS EMPLOYEES. THE LAST ONE GOT FIRED FOR WEARING CULOTTES ON CASUAL DAY.

IT WAS SUCH A GOOD IDEA IN MY HEAD.

WE STILL HAVE SOME SARCASTIC EMPLOYEES. CAN YOU WORK WITH THAT?

WE'VE IDENTIFIED THE PEOPLE WHO WILL CREATE THE SYSTEM TO DEVELOP A PRODUCT PROCESS.

WHILE WE WERE DOING THAT, OUR COMPETITOR CREATED A NEW INTERNET PRODUCT THAT ADDED A BILLION DOLLARS TO THEIR STOCK VALUE.

EXPERTS ATTRIBUTE THE COMPANY'S SUCCESS TO THEIR "EMPLOYEE OF THE WEEK" PROGRAM.

QUICK! HIRE THOSE EXPERTS!

I'M PUTTING YOU ON A "NEED TO KNOW" BASIS.

HERE'S A COMPLETE LIST OF THE THINGS I NEED TO KNOW. IF IT'S NOT ON THE LIST, I PROBABLY DON'T NEED TO HEAR IT.

NUMBER ONE: "RUN FOR IT, DOGBERT! THE VOLCANO IS ERUPTING!"

PLURALS WILL ALSO BE ALLOWED.

IF THE GOAL OF ALL CREATURES IS TO BE HAPPY... AND I'M HAPPIER THAN YOU ARE...

WE CAN CONCLUDE THAT I'M MORE SUCCESSFUL THAN YOU ARE. ISN'T THAT RIGHT?

YOU ARE REALLY STARTING TO ANNOY ME NOW.

THE GAP WIDENS.

YES!

I FINALLY FIGURED OUT WHY EVERYONE TALKS SO FUNNY IN THIS COMPANY.

WE'RE NOT MORONS WHO ARE INCAPABLE OF CLEAR COMMUNICATION. WE'RE REBELS WHO LIKE TO "THINK OUTSIDE THE BOX."

IT'S ALWAYS FASCINATING TO WATCH AN EGO JUST BEFORE IT DIES.

I'M A REBEL! TASK ME WITH A "DO IT."

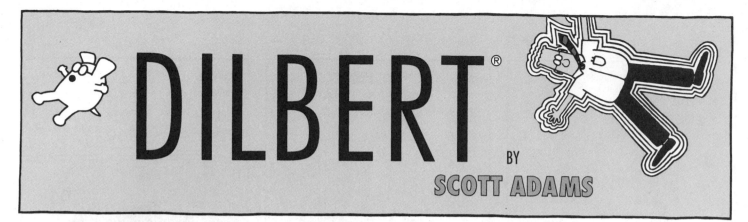

DILBERT

BY **SCOTT ADAMS**

HEY, POINTY-HAIR!

THANKS FOR YOUR BRILLIANT ADVICE THAT I SHOULD, "WORK SMARTER NOT HARDER."

I DIDN'T REALIZE PEOPLE COULD BECOME SMARTER JUST BY WANTING TO.

WATCH ME ADD A FEW IQ POINTS RIGHT NOW!

GRRR GRRR

WOW! SUDDENLY I CAN SPEAK LATIN!

LET'S CRANK IT UP A FEW MORE POINTS.

GRRR GRRR

WHY AM I WORKING IN THIS DUMP? I SHOULD BE A CONSULTANT.

WHEN I WOKE UP, MY PILLOW WAS GONE.

OH, WOW. YOU WOKE UP IN THE WRONG JOKE.

WOW. YOU'RE AN INCREDIBLY SEXY MAN. IT'S TOO BAD I MET THIS LITTLE FUZZY GUY FIRST.

BUT LOOKS AREN'T EVERYTHING. STUDIES SHOW THAT WOMEN WANT A MAN WHO IS IN TOUCH WITH HIS FEELINGS.

AAGH!! I HATE MY LIFE!!

GEE. THAT'S ENOUGH TO MAKE ME DOUBT THE SCIENTIFIC METHOD.

AS MUCH AS I LIKE THE PETTING, I STILL HAVE TO BREAK UP WITH YOU, ROXANNE.

WHY?!

HUMANS ARE KIND, INTELLIGENT, WELL-ADJUSTED CREATURES

UNTIL YOU GET TO KNOW THEM.

MAY THE HORNED DEMONS OF IXPAH SMITE YOU LIKE THE LAST SIX!!!

THIS IS WHAT I'M TALKING ABOUT.

IT'S DONE.

I THOUGHT I ASKED FOR THAT TO BE IN COLOR.

BLACK AND WHITE ARE BOTH COLORS. SO TECHNICALLY... OH, WAIT, I SEE WHAT YOU MEAN.

IS THAT ALL IT TOOK TO SATISFY HIS NEED FOR IRRELEVANT CHANGES?

AND I DID IT WHILE THE COLOR COPIES WERE PRINTING.

DILBERT®

BY SCOTT ADAMS

YOU'RE ON THE RADIO WITH DOGBERT'S "BAD ADVICE SHOW." HOW MAY I HURT YOU?

MY BOSS ASKED ME FOR A DATE. WE'RE BOTH MARRIED. WHAT SHOULD I DO?

DIVORCE YOUR HUSBAND. HE SOUNDS LIKE A LOSER TO ME.

YES, YES, IT ALL MAKES SENSE WHEN YOU EXPLAIN IT THAT WAY.

THEN MAIL A DEAD WOODCHUCK TO YOUR BOSS WITH A NOTE THAT SAYS...

"UNLIKE THIS WOODCHUCK, MY LOVE FOR YOU WILL NEVER DIE."

THANKS. I LOVE YOUR SHOW.

MOVING ON TO HOUSE-HOLD TIPS, DID YOU KNOW THAT BLACK PAINT IS AN EXCELLENT STAIN REMOVER?

CAN WE TALK?

... AND THOSE ARE JUST SOME OF THE BENEFITS OF AN ALL-CHEESE DIET.

I'VE BEEN ASKED TO GIVE A PRESENTATION AT THE TRADE SHOW.

I'D LIKE YOU TO PUT THAT TOGETHER FOR ME, ALICE.

WHAT'S YOUR TOPIC?

TECHNOLOGY. THEY DIDN'T SAY IF I'M FOR IT OR AGAINST IT.

I'LL LEAVE SOME WIGGLE ROOM.

I'VE PREPARED YOUR POINTLESS PRESENTATION FOR THE TRADE SHOW.

IT'S GOT THE USUAL TIME-WASTING FILLER: A GRAPHIC OF MOORE'S LAW, A "NETSCAPE" COMPARISON, AND IRONICALLY...

...IT ENDS WITH AN IMPASSIONED REMINDER TO THINK IN NEW WAYS.

MAYBE I SHOULD GIVE OUT SOME AWARDS, TOO.

I ONLY HAVE THIRTY MINUTES AND HE'S BABBLED FOR TWENTY-EIGHT.

BLAH BLAH BLAH

IT TOOK THREE WEEKS TO GET ON HIS CALENDAR. MY ONLY HOPE IS TO SEND ESP MESSAGES FOR HIM TO SHUT UP.

SHUT UP SHUT UP SHUT UP SHUT UP SHUT UP

NICE TRY, BUT IT'S TIME FOR HIS NEXT FILIBUSTER.

BLAH BLAH BLAH

TEN OF OUR FINEST EXECUTIVES GOT TOGETHER AND CREATED A STATEMENT OF OUR CORE VALUES.

"WE HELP THE COMMUNITY AND THE WORLD BY PRODUCING STATE-OF-THE-ART BUSINESS SOLUTIONS."

I'M GLAD WE DIDN'T SKIMP AND TRY TO DO THAT WITH ONLY NINE EXECUTIVES.

YEAH. IT MIGHT HAVE SUCKED.

CAN YOU EXPLAIN HOW THE COMPANY'S NEW "STATEMENT OF CORE VALUES" WILL CHANGE MY BEHAVIOR?

I WAS PLANNING TO POISON THE TOWN'S WATER SUPPLY.

BUT WAIT! IT'S AGAINST OUR CORE VALUES!

IS YOUR SARCASM ABSOLUTELY NECESSARY?

LET ME CHECK. HMM... IT'S NOT ADDRESSED.

GIVE ME THE NAME OF ANY FAMOUS PERSON.

SANDRA BULLOCK.

SANDRA BULLOCK WAS IN A MOVIE WITH KEVIN SPACEY... AND KEVIN SPACEY EATS BACON.

SEE THAT? EVERYONE ON EARTH IS ONLY ONE DEGREE AWAY FROM SOMEONE NAMED KEVIN WHO EATS BACON!

THAT IS SO CLOSE TO BEING FASCINATING.

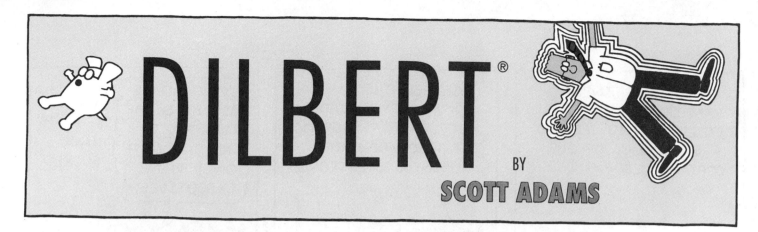

HERE'S THE AGENDA. THE FIRST HOUR WILL BE U.B.R., AS USUAL.

THIS REMINDS ME OF MY FIRST JOB, BEFORE CRASH DUMMIES WERE POPULAR. MAN, I SPENT A FORTUNE ON ASPIRIN.

WHAT EXACTLY IS U.B.R.?

UNFOCUSED BOSS RAMBLING. ONLY 58 MINUTES TO GO.

...AND THAT'S YOUR PERFORMANCE REVIEW. ANY QUESTIONS?

ONE.

YOU TALKED ABOUT YOURSELF FOR THE FULL HOUR. CAN WE TALK ABOUT ME?

OKAY. **YOU** DON'T SEEM TO KNOW THAT **YOUR** MEETING IS OVER WHEN **YOU** SEE ME STAND UP.

OOH.

CATBERT: EVIL H.R. DIRECTOR

I CAN'T ABUSE PEOPLE IF THEY QUIT THE COMPANY. I'D BETTER FIND A WAY TO REDUCE TURNOVER.

ALL JOB TITLES WILL BE CHANGED AS FOLLOWS...

MY NEW TITLE IS... "CONVICTED FELON."

THAT'LL LOOK GOOD ON THE OL' RÉSUMÉ.

OUR NEW JOB TITLES FROM HUMAN RESOURCES ARE DEMEANING AND INSULTING!

YOU'VE GOT TO USE YOUR MANAGERIAL INFLUENCE TO DO SOMETHING!

MY NEW CARD...

HOW'D IT GO?

I DON'T EXPECT MUCH HELP FROM THE "DIRECTOR OF LEARNED HELPLESSNESS."

WISH ME LUCK.

FOR WHAT?

I'M GOING TO FIND PEOPLE WHO LAUGH NERVOUSLY EVERY TIME THEY TALK. THEN I'LL SMACK THEM WITH MY FLYSWATTER.

AND THE REASON WOULD BE?

IT WOULDN'T BE A HOBBY IF IT HAD A REASON.

ALICE, I FOUND THIS ARTICLE IN A MAGAZINE.

I HIGHLIGHTED THE MOST IMPORTANT STUFF TO SAVE YOU TIME.

YOU HIGHLIGHTED THE PAGE NUMBERS.

IT TAKES FOREVER IF YOU DON'T NOTICE THOSE.

DILBERT®

BY SCOTT ADAMS

WHAT IF...

ALBERT EINSTEIN HAD BEEN IN MARKETING?

I HAVE A GREAT IDEA FOR INCREASING SALES.

NOPE. THIS WILL NEVER WORK.

UM... IS IT POSSIBLE THAT YOU DON'T FULLY UNDERSTAND THE IDEA?

THAT'S QUITE AN EGO YOU HAVE THERE, ALLAN.

ALBERT.

EXPERIENCED MANAGERS KNOW HOW TO IDENTIFY BAD IDEAS...

BAD IDEAS COME FROM OTHER PEOPLE.

NOW GO WORK SMARTER, NOT HARDER.

I WORRY THAT A GUY LIKE THAT WILL GO OFF AND BUILD A HUGE BOMB.

GREAT NEWS! OUR STRONGEST COMPETITOR OFFERED TO SELL US THEIR PRODUCT LINE.

OBVIOUSLY THEY THINK THEIR PRODUCTS ARE NOT VIABLE. WE'D HAVE TO BE AMAZINGLY STUPID...

AND YOU'LL BE IN CHARGE OF INTEGRATING THEIR PRODUCT LINE WITH OURS.

...TO WORK HERE.

TELL ME THE TRUTH. USE THE ENGINEER'S SECRET CODE IF YOU MUST.

ARE THERE ANY LITTLE PROBLEMS WITH THE TECHNOLOGY THAT MY MANAGERS AGREED TO BUY FROM YOUR COMPANY?

HA HA SNORT SNORT HA HA HA !!!

1100111... GOOD. GO ON.

IT'S MY JOB TO INTEGRATE THE BAD TECHNOLOGY THAT OUR IDIOT BOSS BOUGHT WITH THE GOOD TECHNOLOGY WE ALREADY OWN. YOUR ADVICE?

THROW AWAY THE BAD TECHNOLOGY. GOOF OFF UNTIL THE NEXT PLANNED UPGRADE OF THE GOOD TECHNOLOGY. TELL YOUR BOSS THE IMPROVEMENTS ARE A RESULT OF HIS BRILLIANT BUYING DECISION.

WOW. THAT'S ALMOST PURE EVIL.

YOU'RE WELCOME.

 # DILBERT

BY **SCOTT ADAMS**

WELCOME TO THE EMPLOYEE ROCK-CLIMBING SEMINAR.

YOU'LL LEARN VALUABLE TEAMWORK SKILLS BY DOING DANGEROUS THINGS UNRELATED TO YOUR JOBS.

ISN'T ROCK CLIMBING A SOLO ACTIVITY?

I'LL HELP IDENTIFY YOUR BODY.

IT SEEMS LIKE YOU'D NEED A STRONG GRIP TO CLIMB ROCKS.

I CAN'T EVEN OPEN JARS UNLESS I USE SPECIAL TOOLS.

OW! OW! CRAMP!!

I'M DISORIENTED BY THE PAIN!

HEY!

HERE ARE YOUR DIPLOMAS. NOW GET OUT.

GO TEAM!

I'M IN CHARGE OF THE OFFICE RELOCATION. WHERE DO YOU WANT YOUR CUBICLE?

WHAT'S THIS HUGE STRUCTURE?

WALLYVILLE. IT'S TWO FLOORS OF LUXURY HOUSING, SHOPPING, AND GAMBLING.

DO YOU THINK YOU MIGHT BE ABUSING YOUR POWER?

WHAT WOULD BE THE OTHER REASONS TO HAVE POWER?

ACCORDING TO THE BLUEPRINTS, YOUR NEW CUBICLE HAS A SUPPORT BEAM IN IT.

AT LEAST I HAVE A WINDOW VIEW.

IT'S 108° BY THE WINDOW. BUT AT LEAST THERE'S A BREEZE FROM THE PEOPLE WHO WALK BY AND LAUGH.

DON'T LET ME SLOW YOUR SEARCH FOR SOMEONE WHO'S INTERESTED.

WE'RE GOING TO TRY SOMETHING CALLED "OPEN BOOK MANAGEMENT."

WE'LL TEACH YOU TO READ THE FINANCIAL STATEMENTS OF THIS COMPANY. IT'S ALL VERY MOTIVATING.

...AND OUR CEO GOT PAID MORE THAN THE ENTIRE CAPITAL BUDGET...

IS THIS WHAT MOTIVATION FEELS LIKE?

OPEN BOOK MANAGEMENT

SO YOU SEE, IF YOU GOT A RAISE, OUR EARNINGS GROWTH WOULDN'T BE SMOOTH.

AND SMOOTH EARNINGS ARE GOOD FOR WHO?

STOCK MARKET ANALYSTS?

SPECIFICALLY, THE LAZY ONES.

I'M FINE, NOW THAT I UNDERSTAND.

I APPRECIATE YOUR NEW "OPEN BOOK MANAGEMENT" PHILOSOPHY...

FOR EXAMPLE, I'VE LEARNED THAT WE'RE REPURCHASING STOCK WHILE I'M WORKING UNPAID OVERTIME.

YET I REMAIN HIGHLY MOTIVATED BECAUSE I UNDERSTAND THAT INCOME AND EQUITY ARE DISTINCT CONCEPTS.

WHO SAID IGNORANCE IS BLISS? HA!

OPEN BOOK MANAGEMENT

...THEN I SEZ, "HEY OUR DEBT TO EQUITY RATIO IS INCREASING."

I LEAPT INTO ACTION AND STARTED SWEEPING LIKE I'VE NEVER SWEPT BEFORE!

THEN I SEZ, "HEY, WHY AM I USING A BROOM ON CARPETS?"

DILBERT
BY
SCOTT ADAMS

ANNOUNCING PROJECT "SPARKLE," THE CLEAN DESK POLICY.

THIS IS A COMPANY-WIDE EFFORT TO KEEP OUR WORK SPACES CLEAN.

TINY QUESTION. I'M CURIOUS ABOUT ONE THING.

I'M PICTURING OUR TOP EXECUTIVES IN THE "WAR ROOM."

THEY TALK ABOUT THE COMPETITIVE THREAT AND OUR LACK OF RESOURCES. SUDDENLY, PANIC SETS IN!!

A LONE VOICE OF REASON PENETRATES THE CONFUSION. TWO WORDS: "PAPER TOWELS."

IS THAT PRETTY MUCH HOW IT WENT?

MOVING ALONG, YOU EACH GET A LAMINATED CARD WITH OUR MISSION STATEMENT.

LET ME DO THIS ONE.

I HAVE A NEW METHOD FOR BLOWING OFF THE IDIOTS WHO ASK QUESTIONS.

I SAY, "THAT INFORMATION IS ON MY WEB PAGE. SHOO, SHOO."

WHAT HAPPENS WHEN THEY FIND OUT IT ISN'T?

I'LL SAY, "YOU MUST HAVE MISUNDERSTOOD YOUR QUESTION."

CATBERT: EVIL H.R. DIRECTOR

HERE'S THE NEW "CLEAN DESK" POLICY, WALLY.

"EMPLOYEES MUST LICK THEIR WORK-PLACES CLEAN AT THE END OF EACH BUSINESS DAY."

DO THEY SERIOUSLY THINK WE'RE THIS SPINELESS AND STUPID?

AHM NAH CHANTHING IT.

THERE'S A RUMOR THE COMPANY IS MOVING TO SOUTH DAKOTA FOR TAX REASONS.

DO YOU SERIOUSLY THINK THEY WOULD DISRUPT THE LIVES OF THOUSANDS OF EMPLOYEES JUST TO SAVE MONEY ON TAXES?

I THINK THEY'D KILL US IN OUR SLEEP AND SELL OUR ORGANS IF THE RETURN ON INVESTMENT WAS GOOD.

STOP IT. I'LL BE AFRAID TO SLEEP IN MY CUBICLE NOW.

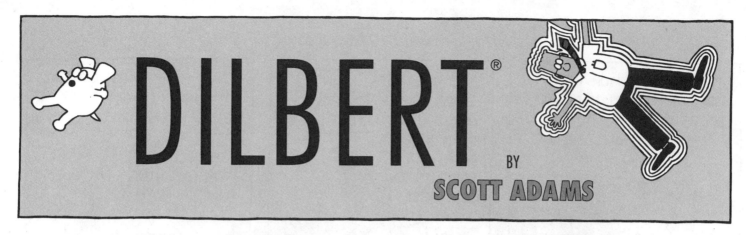

DILBERT® BY SCOTT ADAMS

I HAVE A VAGUE FEELING OF UNCERTAINTY.

IT GETS STRONGER AT THE OFFICE.

THE UNCERTAINTY SAPS MY STRENGTH. MY BRIEFCASE IS GETTING HEAVIER.

MUST... GET... TO... CUBICLE.

THE UNCERTAINTY FEELS LIKE A PIANO UPON MY CHEST.

I DECIDED TO REORGANIZE. OR MAYBE DOWNSIZE. UNLESS THERE'S A MERGER.

MMPH MMPH

I SUMMON THE UNHOLY DEMONS OF APATHY, SARCASM AND CYNICISM!!

GOOD THINKING! REORGANIZATIONS ALWAYS INCREASE PROFITS!

WOW. THIRD TIME TODAY.

DILBERT

BY SCOTT ADAMS

WE HAVE THE RESULTS OF THE EMPLOYEE COMMUNICATIONS SURVEY.

THE NUMBER ONE PROBLEM IS "FEAR OF GIVING NEGATIVE NEWS TO MANAGERS."

Negative News

WHAT?! WHY HAVEN'T I HEARD THIS BEFORE?

WELL... MAYBE BECAUSE IT'S NEGATIVE NEWS?

DO YOU HAVE A SOLUTION OR DID YOU JUST COME TO INSULT ME?

DON'T GET INVOLVED.

OOH. UM... MAYBE IF WE WAIT A FEW DAYS IT WILL TAKE CARE OF ITSELF.

FINE. NEXT.

HAPPILY, THERE ARE NO OTHER COMMUNICATION PROBLEMS WHATSOEVER.

HEH HEH.

I WONDER WHY SO MANY PROBLEMS GO AWAY ON THEIR OWN.

I HAVE NO COMMENT AT THIS TIME.

CATBERT: EVIL H.R. DIRECTOR

ALICE YOU HAVE TO USE YOUR VACATION TIME OR YOU'LL LOSE IT.

BUT IF YOU TAKE TIME OFF, YOU'LL MISS YOUR DEADLINES. **HA HA HA HA HA HA!!!**

THIS IS EMBARRASSING. I LAUGHED MYSELF FUZZY.

IT'S A SHAME YOU HAVE TO WORK DURING YOUR VACATION. THE SAME THING HAPPENED TO ME.

REALLY?

ACTUALLY, IN MY CASE I WENT ON VACATION WHEN I WAS SUPPOSED TO BE WORKING. BUT THE CONCEPT IS THE SAME.

APPARENTLY SHE WASN'T LOOKING FOR EMPATHY.

I ADMIRE YOUR WORK ETHIC, ALICE. YOU'RE EVEN WORKING DURING YOUR VACATION.

IT MUST BE HARD TO REMAIN MOTIVATED WHEN YOU KNOW YOU CAN NEVER BREAK THROUGH THE GLASS CEILING.

SO, IT LOOKS LIKE IT'S JUST TILE AFTER ALL.

I'M GOING BACK TO MY OLD JOB AS A NETWORK SYSTEMS ADMINISTRATOR.

WHY?

I'M ATTRACTED BY THE POTENTIAL FOR RECKLESS ABUSE OF POWER.

CHIPS

THIS NEW ETHERNET CARD COULD SOLVE YOUR PROBLEM. WOULD YOU LIKE A SNIFF BEFORE I THROW IT IN A BIG PILE IN MY OFFICE?

DOGBERT THE NETWORK SYSTEMS ADMINISTRATOR

THE SOFTWARE MANUALS ARE LOCKED IN THIS ROOM.

I DON'T LET USERS HAVE MANUALS, FOR REASONS THAT COULD ONLY BE DESCRIBED AS MEAN-SPIRITED.

IS THERE ANY WAY WE CAN MEET HALF-WAY ON THIS?

HEY, THAT DOOR DIDN'T ALWAYS HAVE A WINDOW.

DOGBERT THE NETWORK SYSTEMS ADMINISTRATOR

WALLY, DID YOU KNOW YOUR E-MAIL SYSTEM ISN'T PRIVATE?

I'VE COMPILED A BINDER WITH ALL OF YOUR OFF-COLOR HUMOR, UNKIND REFERENCES TO CO-WORKERS, NAUGHTY PROPOSITIONS, AND ADMISSIONS OF THEFT.

WHERE IS THIS HEADING?

I'D LIKE YOU TO SING THAT QUESTION WHILE HOPPING ON ONE FOOT.

"THIS IS DOGBERT THE NETWORK SYSTEMS ADMINISTRATOR, TO ALL IGNORANT EMPLOYEES."

HE WHO CONTROLS YOUR INFORMATION CONTROLS YOU. I CONTROL YOUR INFORMATION.

"THE BOARD OF DIRECTORS HAS APPOINTED ME EMPEROR FOR LIFE. BRING THE POINTY-HAIRED BOSS TO ME."

UH-OH! THE ESCAPE KEY ISN'T WORKING!

DOGBERT: COMPANY EMPEROR

TELL THE EMPLOYEES TO GET WHEELBARROWS TO CARRY MY SALARY OUT OF HERE.

TURN OUT THE LIGHTS WHEN YOU'RE DONE. YOU'RE ALL DOWNSIZED. SHOO!

THE MEDIA LOVED HIM

CAN WE CALL YOU "BUZZ SAW DOGBERT"?

I BOUGHT YOUR PARENT COMPANY TODAY. YOU'RE DOWNSIZED. SHOO!

DOGBERT: CORPORATE EMPEROR

I DON'T LIKE TO CALL WHAT I'M DOING "DOWNSIZING." IT SOUNDS TOO NEGATIVE.

I LIKE TO CALL IT "WEDGIESIZING." NOW CLEAN OUT YOUR DESK AND SHOO!

YANK!

HE DIDN'T TAKE THAT VERY WELL.

YOU CAN'T PLEASE EVERYONE, BOB.

DILBERT BY SCOTT ADAMS

THIS IS DOGBERT'S TECHNICAL SUPPORT. HOW MAY I DISCONNECT YOU?

WHAT ARE MY CHOICES?

I RECOMMEND THE ABRUPT DISCONNECT; SIMPLE, GETS THE JOB DONE.

I HAD THAT LAST TIME. WHAT ELSE DO YOU HAVE?

YOU MIGHT LIKE OUR "PLEASE HOLD," FOLLOWED BY THE "WRONG BUTTON," DISCONNECT.

TOO PREDICTABLE. DO YOU HAVE ANYTHING NEW?

TRY OUR "KEVORKIAN DISCONNECT." I PUT YOU ON HOLD AND PLAY AN ANNOYING MESSAGE UNTIL YOU DISCONNECT YOURSELF.

YOUR CALL IS IMPORTANT. PLEASE HOLD WHILE WE IGNORE IT ... YOUR CALL IS IMPORTANT...

NOT BAD.

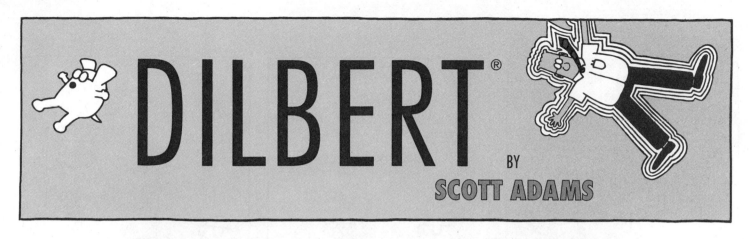

DILBERT®

BY SCOTT ADAMS

CAROL, I FORGET... HOW DO I ADDRESS AN ENVELOPE?

I'LL DO IT.

I'M TRAINING HIM TO BE HELPLESS.

IT'S PART OF MY MASTER PLAN TO ELIMINATE HIM.

I DO EVERYTHING FOR HIM. SOON HE'LL LOSE HIS ABILITY TO SOLVE SMALL PROBLEMS ALONE.

THEN I'LL "ACCIDENTALLY" BOOK HIM ON A ONE-WAY TRIP TO SOUTH KOREA.

BEFORE HE GOES, I'LL TELL HIM THEY HAVE A DEATH PENALTY FOR SPEAKING ENGLISH.

WE'LL NEVER SEE HIM AGAIN. BUWAHAHA!!!

IT'S WORTH A SHOT.

CAROL, WHAT DO I DIAL FOR AN OUT-SIDE LINE?

I'LL DO IT.

I AM MORDAC THE REFUSER. I AM HERE TO DISCUSS YOUR REQUEST FOR A COMPUTER UPGRADE.

CRINKLE!

MMPHH!

CHOMP   CHOMP

CHOMP

WE LOTHT THUH PAHPER-WUHK.

THAT'S A HUGE SURPRISE. LUCKILY I MADE SEVENTY-FIVE EXTRA COPIES.

I AM MORDAC THE PREVENTER, YOUR LIAISON FROM THE INFORMATION TECHNOLOGY DEPARTMENT.

I COME WITH TALES OF RESOURCE SHORTAGES. YOUR REQUEST FOR OUR SERVICES IS DENIED.

I DIDN'T REQUEST ANY OF YOUR SERVICES.

DON'T TRY YOUR REVERSE PSYCHOLOGY ON ME.

I'M NOT USING REVERSE PSYCHOLOGY! I REALLY DON'T NEED ANYTHING FROM THE INFORMATION TECHNOLOGY DEPARTMENT.

CURSE YOU! YOU KNOW OUR GOAL IS TO GIVE YOU THE OPPOSITE OF WHAT YOU WANT. IF YOU WANT NOTHING WE MUST GIVE YOU EVERYTHING!

PLEASE TELL ME HOW YOU GOT THEM TO DO THIS.

WATCH ME LAUNCH THE SPACE SHUTTLE!

FOR THOSE WHO JOINED US LATE, THIS IS BOB THE DINOSAUR. HE LIVES WITH DILBERT AND ME.

HI

DINOSAURS AREN'T EXTINCT. THEY'RE JUST HIDING BEHIND FURNITURE

THIS IS DAWN, MY MATE, AND LITTLE REX.

YOU'LL NOTICE THAT THEY USE A LOT OF SPACE AND THEY AREN'T VERY RELEVANT.

I THINK REX HAS MY EYES.

THERE'S NOT ENOUGH ROOM FOR ALL OF YOU DINOSAURS. ONE OF YOU MUST BE DOWNSIZED.

IF IT HELPS, THESE SPIKEY THINGS ARE A SAFETY HAZARD. AND LITTLE REX ATE YOUR FICUS TREE.

THANKS FOR BEING PROFESSIONAL ABOUT THIS, BOB.

WHEN YOU PUT HIM IN GOOD LIGHT, HOW CUTE IS HE REALLY?

SHOULD THE DINOSAURS BE DOWNSIZED? YOU DECIDE THEIR FATE.

VOTE BY E-MAIL:
DINOSAURS@UNITEDMEDIA.COM

A. I LOVE THE DINOSAURS!
B. STICK TO OFFICE JOKES!
C. NO TALKING ANIMALS!
D. I DON'T HAVE ANY OPINIONS BUT I LIKE TO VOTE!
E. GET RID OF EVERYONE SO I CAN USE THE BLANK SPACE FOR NOTES.

THERE'S A JIMMY CARTER HERE TO MONITOR THE VOTING.

UH-OH.

LOOK AT THE "ROLEX" WATCH I GOT FROM A VENDOR.

DO YOU KNOW THERE'S A CORPORATE LIMIT OF FIFTY DOLLARS FOR VENDOR GIFTS?

SURE.

AND YOU KNOW THAT'S A MAXIMUM NOT A MINIMUM.

OOH. MAYBE THAT'S WHY HE WHINED WHEN I TOOK IT OFF HIS ARM.

DO YOU REALIZE THIS IS OUR THIRD DATE?

WE'RE NOT DATING. I'M A VENDOR AND YOU'RE MY CLIENT.

YOU ALWAYS SAY THE ONLY TIME WE CAN MEET IS DURING LUNCH. THAT WAY I'M OBLIGATED TO PAY FOR IT.

YOU'RE FEISTY. I'D BETTER GET THE OYSTERS.

MAKE SALE FIRST. THEN KILL CLIENT.

I'M PUTTING YOU IN CHARGE OF GETTING ISO 14000 CERTIFICATION.

WHAT'S THE DIFFERENCE BETWEEN THAT AND ISO 9000?

OH, ABOUT 6000. HA HA HA HA!!

HEY, I THINK I'LL USE THAT ONE AT THE STOCKHOLDER MEETING!

YEAH, THAT'LL WAKE THEM UP.

I UNDERSTAND IT'S YOUR JOB TO MAKE SURE YOUR COMPANY CAN PASS AN ISO 14000 INSPECTION.

AND I UNDERSTAND THAT YOUR COMPANY PAYS THE INSPECTOR FOR EACH INSPECTION.

SO?

DOGBERT: ISO 14000 INSPECTOR

YOU FAIL AGAIN. THAT'S $10,000 PLEASE.

NEXT TIME, COULD YOU ACTUALLY WALK AROUND AND LOOK AT STUFF?

I DIDN'T USE MY BRAIN THIS WEEK.

I LISTENED TO THINGS I ALREADY KNEW; I WAITED FOR PEOPLE WHO WERE LATE; I WAS A PASSENGER IN MY CAR POOL.

LET'S START THE STAFF MEETING.

YES!! KEEPING THE STREAK ALIVE!

WE HAVE TO IMPROVE OUR IMAGE IN THE INTERNET COMMUNITY.

LET'S DO A MASS UNSOLICITED E-MAIL CAMPAIGN TO TELL PEOPLE HOW NICE WE ARE.

YOU HAVE THE LOOK OF A MAN WHO WAS JUST PUT IN CHARGE OF IMPLEMENTING HIS OWN SARCASTIC SUGGESTION.

DILBERT®

BY

SCOTT ADAMS

GET MY APPROVAL AT EACH PHASE. FINISH IN ONE MONTH.

LET'S SEE... YOU'RE ON VACATION NEXT WEEK. THEN YOU'RE TRAVELING. THEN THERE'S YOUR EXECUTIVE RETREAT...

... IT TAKES THREE WEEKS TO GET ON YOUR CALENDAR... AND THE PROJECT HAS SIX PHASES...

WHAT WE HAVE HERE IS GUARANTEED FAILURE.

YOU'VE LEFT NOTHING TO CHANCE ON THIS ONE.

I MEAN, NORMALLY THERE'S A BIT OF UNCERTAINTY, BUT YOU'VE... OH.

YOU'VE SLIPPED INTO THE "BOSS ZONE" WHERE YOU CAN'T SEE OR HEAR EMPLOYEE INPUT.

IT'S WEIRD. I LOST TEN MINUTES, AND WHEN I WOKE UP, MY DOUGHNUTS WERE GONE.

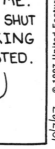

DILBERT

BY **SCOTT ADAMS**

I HAVE TO MAKE A QUICK PHONE CALL.

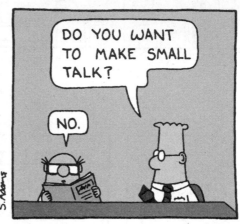

DO YOU WANT TO MAKE SMALL TALK?

NO.

I BROUGHT A MAGAZINE.

COULD YOU TEAR OUT A FEW PAGES FOR ME TO READ?

THAT WOULDN'T BE RIGHT.

GIVE ME SOME PAGES OR ELSE I'LL ASK ALICE ABOUT PANTY HOSE.

YOU WOULDN'T DARE.

SO, ALICE, WHAT DO YOU THINK OF THE CONCEPT OF PANTY HOSE?

AARGH!! WHAT MORON INVENTED LEG COVERS THAT CAN BE DESTROYED BY TOUCHING A TWIG?!

HERE! MAKE IT STOP!!

TOO LATE.

LOOK AT THIS!!!!

DOGBERT MUTUAL FUND

I DON'T UNDERSTAND WHY ANY INTELLIGENT INVESTOR WOULD PUT MONEY IN A FUND THAT HAS NO TRACK RECORD.

I TRY TO STEER CLEAR OF INTELLIGENT INVESTORS.

HERE'S MY LIFE'S SAVINGS.

DO YOU WANT MY NAME AND ADDRESS?

NO, I TRUST YOU.

THE DOGBERT MUTUAL FUND

IS IT HARD TO WRITE AN EARNINGS REPORT AFTER YOU STEAL THE INVESTORS' MONEY?

NAH.

I'LL JUST COMPARE MY FUND'S PERFORMANCE TO THE S&P 500 UNDER A COMMON SET OF ASSUMPTIONS.

OH.

HOW DID OUR DOGBERT FUND DO?

"TEN PERCENT BETTER THAN THE S&P 500 IF IT WERE ALSO MANAGED BY AN UNSCRUPULOUS DOG!"

MY GUEST TODAY ON "MONEY CHATTER" IS THE HEAD OF THE "DOGBERT MUTUAL FUND."

IT'S REPORTED THAT YOUR FUND IS THE HIGHEST PERFORMER OF THE DECADE. TELL US HOW YOU MADE THAT HAPPEN.

OKAY.

APPARENTLY, THIS GUY WILL READ ANYTHING YOU HAND HIM.

DILBERT®

BY SCOTT ADAMS

CATBERT: THE EVIL DIRECTOR OF HUMAN RESOURCES

YOU'RE NEXT.

VICTIMS

WALLY

WALLY, YOU'VE BEEN RANDOMLY SELECTED FOR AN EMPLOYEE DRUG TEST.

RANDOMLY? WHY AM I THE ONLY ONE WHO GETS PICKED EVERY WEEK?!

YOU'RE VERY UNLUCKY AT WORK. BUT I'M SURE YOU COMPENSATE BY BEING LUCKY AT LOVE.

HA HA HA HA HA HA

ANYWAY... OUR NEW DRUG TEST USES HAIR SAMPLES...

TO BE SAFE, GIVE ME SIX HAIRS... AND ONE WHOLE EYEBROW.

I'LL COME BACK IN AN HOUR AND SAY I LOST THE BOX.

PURR PURR PURR

I'M GOING INTO THE SPORTS MEMORABILIA BUSINESS.

I'VE HEARD THAT MOST AUTOGRAPHS ARE FORGERIES, SO MY INITIAL INVESTMENT WILL BE LOW.

CAN I INTEREST YOU IN A BASEBALL SIGNED BY MOSES?

WOW! THAT'S GOING TO BE WORTH SOMETHING.

SPORTS MEMORABILIA

THIS IS THE BEST PRICE I'VE SEEN FOR A BASEBALL AUTOGRAPHED BY BABE RUTH.

BUT I DON'T SEE WHERE THE AUTOGRAPH IS.

IT GETS AUTOGRAPHED LATER TONIGHT.

I'LL TAKE THIS AND THREE OF THE HONUS WAGNER CARDS.

YOU SAY THIS FOOTBALL WAS AUTOGRAPHED BY JESUS...

BUT I'M NO FOOL. THIS ISN'T A FOOTBALL. IT HAS NO STITCHES.

THEY HEALED.

WOW!

AND I THINK I HEARD IT OINK.

AUTOGRAPHS FOR SALE

WOW... A SOFTBALL SIGNED BY MARTIN LUTHER, LEADER OF THE PROTESTANT REFORMATION.

I'M IMPRESSED, BUT WHAT I'M LOOKING FOR IS SOMETHING SIGNED BY MARTIN LUTHER <u>KING</u> <u>JR</u>.

TOO BAD YOU DON'T HAVE ANYTHING FROM HIM.

CHECK BACK IN TEN MINUTES.

IF YOU WANT TO BE PROMOTED, YOU HAVE TO BE HIGHLY VISIBLE.

ASK QUESTIONS AT MEETINGS. BUT MAKE THEM EASY SO YOU DON'T EMBARRASS YOUR BOSS.

...SO IF THERE'S AN ACCIDENT IN A COMPANY CAR, WHERE SHOULD WE BURY THE SURVIVORS?

I USUALLY PUT THEM IN THE TRUNK.

I'VE BEEN SEEING A BEAUTIFUL WOMAN. BUT SOMETHING CAME BETWEEN US.

HER CURTAINS?

VENETIAN BLINDS. TOTALLY UNFORGIVING.

MAYBE SHE GOT SPOOKED WHEN YOU PUT THE LAWN CHAIR IN HER YARD.

DILBERT

BY

SCOTT ADAMS

IT HAS COME TO MY ATTENTION THAT ONE OF YOU HAS A SOCIAL LIFE.

THERE MUST BE SOME MISTAKE.

WE CAN'T BE SUCCESSFUL UNTIL OUR SOCIAL LIVES ARE WORSE THAN THE INDUSTRY AVERAGE.

OUR COMPETITORS SPEND THE NIGHTS IN THEIR CUBICLES. THEY EAT FROM VENDING MACHINES.

SOMEONE HERE HAS NOT SHOWN THE SAME LEVEL OF COMPETITIVE SPIRIT.

SOMEONE HAD A SOCIAL ACTIVITY LAST NIGHT!

I'M SORRY! I THOUGHT THEY WERE FRIENDS... BUT THEY WERE ONLY RECRUITING FOR A MULTI-LEVEL MARKETING NETWORK!!!

WHAT WERE THEY SELLING?

EDIBLE WAX FRUIT...

BROCHURE?

ALICE, I'VE NOTICED A DISTURBING PATTERN. YOUR SOLUTIONS TO PROBLEMS ARE ALWAYS THE THINGS YOU TRY <u>LAST</u>.

WITH ALL DUE RESPECT, ARE YOU USING YOUR SKULL TO STORE OLD RAGS OR WHAT?

IT'S A GOOD THING YOU SAID "WITH ALL DUE RESPECT."

I DISCOVERED THAT OUR POINTY-HAIRED BOSS DOESN'T KNOW HE'S BEING INSULTED IF YOU SAY "WITH ALL DUE RESPECT" FIRST.

I LOVE THE INTANGIBLE BENEFITS OF THIS JOB.

WITH ALL DUE RESPECT, IS THAT YOUR FACE OR IS A MONKEY CLIMBING DOWN YOUR COLLAR HEADFIRST?

CATBERT: EVIL H.R. DIRECTOR

I CAN'T RAISE YOUR SALARY LEVEL BECAUSE YOU DON'T HAVE TEN YEARS EXPERIENCE WITH "JAVA" CODING.

NOBODY HAS TEN YEARS EXPERIENCE WITH NEW TECHNOLOGY! YOU'RE JUST BEING EVIL. ADMIT IT.

AND COULD YOU <u>PLEASE</u> SHAKE YOUR HEAD BACK AND FORTH INSTEAD OF SPINNING IT AROUND?

CATBERT: EVIL H.R. DIRECTOR

THERE ARE SEVERAL MANDATORY CLASSES FOR MANAGERS.

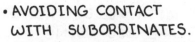

- AVOIDING CONTACT WITH SUBORDINATES.
- MISPLACING IMPORTANT DOCUMENTS.
- THE JOY OF LISTENING TO YOUR OWN VOICE.

HAVE YOU TAKEN THE PREREQUISITE CLASS IN TIME MANAGEMENT?

TWICE.

MANAGER TRAINING

NEVER BE IN THE SAME ROOM AS A DECISION.

DECISION

YOU

I'LL ILLUSTRATE MY POINT WITH A PUPPET SHOW THAT I CALL...

"JOURNEY TO BLAMEVILLE," STARRING "SUGGESTION SAM" AND "MANAGER MEG."

MANAGER TRAINING

YOU WILL OFTEN BE ASKED TO COMMENT ON THINGS YOU DON'T UNDERSTAND.

?

THESE HANDOUTS CONTAIN NONSENSE PHRASES THAT CAN BE USED IN ANY SITUATION.

... SO, LET'S DOMINATE OUR INDUSTRY ... WITH QUALITY IMPLEMENTATION OF METHODOLOGIES.

I'LL GET RIGHT ON IT.

MOST PROBLEMS GO AWAY IF YOU WAIT LONG ENOUGH, ASOK.

IT MIGHT LOOK LIKE I'M STANDING MOTIONLESS, BUT I'M ACTIVELY WAITING FOR OUR PROBLEMS TO GO AWAY.

THERE'S BEEN A REORGANIZATION...

I DON'T KNOW WHY THIS WORKS, BUT IT DOES.

CATBERT: EVIL H.R. DIRECTOR

YOU DON'T NEED TO REWARD EMPLOYEES.

JUST TORTURE THEM LESS. IT WILL FEEL THE SAME AS A REWARD.

YOU MAY SKIP MY STAFF MEETING THIS WEEK, ALICE.

THANK YOU THANK YOU THANK YOU.

WE'LL NEED A RISK ANALYSIS ON THIS PROJECT BEFORE I CAN APPROVE IT.

RISK 1: INDECISIVENESS
RISK 2: OVERANALYSIS
RISK 3: CLUELESSNESS
RISK 4: MICROMANAGE-
       MENT...

CLICK
CLICK
CLICK

I DON'T UNDERSTAND THESE RISKS.

THAT'S NUMBER THIRTY-SIX.

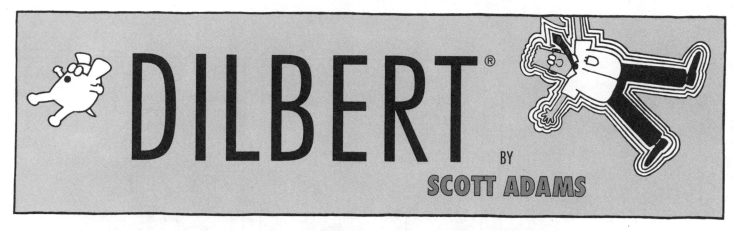

DILBERT®

BY **SCOTT ADAMS**

THE THEME OF OUR ENGINEERING CONFERENCE IS...

"EMPLOYEES ARE OUR MOST VALUABLE ASSET."

AND LIKE MOST ASSETS, YOU DECLINE IN VALUE OVER TIME.

I KNOW WHAT YOU'RE THINKING: NOT ALL ASSETS DECLINE IN VALUE.

FOR EXAMPLE, FINE ART IS WORTH MORE EVERY YEAR.

BUT I DON'T THINK THE LOUVRE WILL BE ASKING FOR ONE OF THESE ANYTIME SOON.

ON YOUR WAY OUT, MISTER CATBERT WILL GIVE EACH OF YOU A CERTIFICATE OF DEPRECIATION.

IT'S STILL BETTER THAN LAST YEAR'S THEME, "HAVE YOU EARNED YOUR AIR TODAY?"

DOGBERT'S DATING ADVICE

WOMEN LIKE MEN WHO HAVE ACCOMPLISHMENTS. BUT THEY HATE MEN WHO BOAST.

I WILL BE YOUR DESIGNATED BRAGGER, ALLOWING YOU TO APPEAR HUMBLE.

ONE POTENTIAL PROBLEM WITH THIS PLAN IS THAT I HAVE NO ACCOMPLISHMENTS.

IF SHE ISN'T WEARING MAKEUP, WE'LL BE HONEST TOO.

HI, DILBERT! HI, DOGBERT!

UH-OH.

SHE'S A HUGGER ON THE FIRST DATE. I NEVER KNOW WHERE MY ARMS SHOULD GO.

I HOPE THIS DOESN'T SEEM AWKWARD, BUT MY WATCH IS SNAGGED ON YOUR BRA STRAP.

I LOVED IT WHEN YOU HUGGED YOUR DATE AND YOUR ARM GOT SNAGGED ON HER BLOUSE...

AND IT WAS HILARIOUS WHEN YOU TRIED TO FREE YOUR ARM AND ACCIDENTALLY RIPPED HER TOP OFF.

BUT THE BEST PART WAS WHEN YOU YELLED, "I'M AN ENGINEER, NOT A DIAMOND CUTTER, DANG IT!"

SHUT UP.

TINA, WE'RE CHANGING THE JOB TITLES OF ALL NON-TECHNICAL PEOPLE.

COLLECTIVELY, YOU'LL BE KNOWN AS OUR S.C.C. GROUP.

I LIKE THE SOUND OF IT — VERY DIGNIFIED. WE WERE BEGINNING TO FEEL LIKE SECOND-CLASS CITIZENS. WHAT'S S.C.C. STAND FOR?

ALL GREAT IDEAS LOOK LIKE BAD IDEAS TO PEOPLE WHO ARE LOSERS.

IT'S ALWAYS GOOD TO TEST A NEW IDEA WITH KNOWN LOSERS TO MAKE SURE THEY DON'T LIKE IT.

DOGBERT'S RESEARCH CO.

WHAT A COINCIDENCE. WE BOTH LOST THREE HOMES IN FLOOD ZONES.

LET'S BEGIN.

DOGBERT RESEARCH CO.

YOU'VE ALL BEEN CARE-FULLY SCREENED FOR THIS FOCUS GROUP.

EACH OF YOU HAS A PATTERN OF MAKING "LOSER CHOICES." I'LL TELL MY CLIENTS TO DO THE OPPOSITE OF WHAT-EVER YOU RECOMMEND.

FUN! I'M GLAD I SKIPPED JURY DUTY TO BE HERE.

I RESCHEDULED MY LIVER TRANS-PLANT!

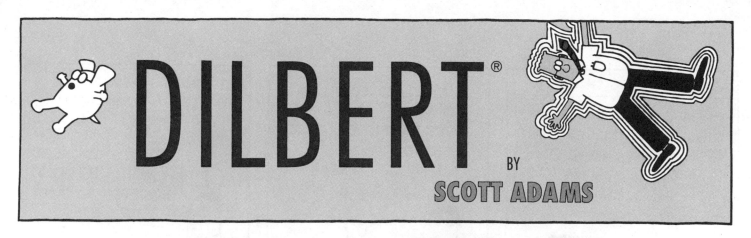

ASOK, AT THIS COMPANY, WE THINK OUR INTERNS ARE AS IMPORTANT AS MINKS TO A MINK COAT.

UM... MINKS DO NOT ENJOY ANY OF THE BENEFITS OF THE MINK COAT.

AND THEY'RE GOOD EATIN', TOO!

I MUST REPORT YOU TO THE ANALOGY POLICE.

ANALOGY POLICE

OPEN

MY BOSS SAID I WAS AS IMPORTANT AS A MINK IS TO A MINK COAT.

THAT SOUNDS FINE TO ME.

BUT THE MINK DIES.

I GUESS YOU WON'T BE LEAVING A FULL FIFTEEN PERCENT TIP.

ARE YOU SURE THIS IS WHERE I REPORT THE MISUSE OF ANALOGIES? YOU'RE DRESSED VERY ODD.

IT'S CASUAL DAY.

THAT'S THE MOST FRIGHTENING OUTFIT I'VE EVER SEEN.

YOU HAVEN'T SEEN ME IN BICYCLE PANTS.

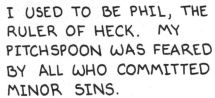
I USED TO BE PHIL, THE RULER OF HECK. MY PITCHSPOON WAS FEARED BY ALL WHO COMMITTED MINOR SINS.

THEN I MADE THE MISTAKE OF MERGING WITH A COMPANY THAT MAKES NON-ALCOHOLIC BEER.

I WAS OUSTED.

THEY SAID WE'D HAVE SYNERGY !!!

MAYBE IT WAS JUST A BAD PUN.

CAN YOU HELP ME WRITE A RÉSUMÉ?

YES, FOR A LARGE FEE.

HOW DO I KNOW YOU'RE QUALIFIED?

CHECK MY RÉSUMÉ.

I'M HAVING TROUBLE BELIEVING THAT YOU INVENTED COFFEE.

CHECK MY PATENT.

CAREER COUNSELING

I'D BE GOOD AT ANY JOB INVOLVING SIN.

PERHAPS SOMETHING IN THE BINGO FIELD... OR MAYBE BUDGET WORK.

HOW ABOUT MARKETING?

I **HAVE** A SOUL. IT'S JUST A SMALL ONE.

GOTCHA. NO MARKETING ... NO AUDITING ... NO GARMENT MANUFACTURING.

DILBERT

BY SCOTT ADAMS

IT IS MY PLEASURE TO PRESENT THE WEEKLY "WALLY STATUS REPORT."

THIS WEEK I DEVELOPED WHAT I CALL "PROCESS PRIDE."

IT ALL STARTED WHEN I REALIZED I HAVE NO IMPACT ON EARNINGS.

OBVIOUSLY I CAN'T TAKE PRIDE IN THE RESULTS OF MY WORK.

OBVIOUSLY.

BUT I NEED PRIDE. OTHERWISE, HOW COULD I MAINTAIN MY HIGH LEVEL OF MORALE?

SO I LEARNED TO TAKE PRIDE IN MY PROCESSES INSTEAD OF MY RESULTS.

EVERYTHING I DO IS STILL POINTLESS, BUT I'M VERY PROUD OF THE WAY I DO IT.

IS THAT ALL YOU DID THIS WEEK?

HEY, I'M ONLY ONE PERSON.

DILBERT®
BY SCOTT ADAMS

WE DON'T HAVE A CUBICLE AVAILABLE FOR YOU YET, BRUCE.

SO I'M DECLARING THIS PART OF THE CARPET TO BE YOUR OFFICE.

IF SOMEONE GOES TO A MEETING, YOU CAN SNEAK INTO HIS CUBICLE AND USE THE PHONE.

OUR COMPUTER BUDGET IS GONE, BUT WE HAVE AN OLD MONITOR THAT YOU CAN PUT ON TOP OF YOUR BRIEFCASE.

CAN I PUT TAPE ON THE CARPET TO MARK MY BOUNDARY?

THAT WON'T BE NECESSARY, THANKS TO THIS HI-TECH DEVICE.

A DOG COLLAR?

IT WILL GIVE A MILD SHOCK IF YOU CROSS YOUR INVISIBLE BOUNDARY.

THE NEW GUY HASN'T LEFT THAT SPOT FOR A WEEK.

WALLY TAUGHT HIM TO BEG FOR FOOD.

DILBERT, I HIRED SOME CONTRACT EMPLOYEES FROM NORTH ELBONIA TO HELP ON YOUR PROJECT.

NORTH ELBONIA IS AN EVIL TOTALITARIAN REGIME. MY PROJECT WILL CREATE TOP SECRET MILITARY TECHNOLOGY TO USE AGAINST THEM.

SURE, BUT YOU HAVE TO WEIGH THAT AGAINST THE FACT THAT THEY'RE WILLING TO WORK FOR FREE.

I'M A LITTLE CONCERNED ABOUT YOUR HIRING COMMUNIST NORTH ELBONIAN CONTRACTORS TO HELP ON MY TOP SECRET MILITARY PROJECT.

DON'T WORRY. WHAT'S THE WORST THING THAT COULD HAPPEN?

I COULD BE EXECUTED FOR TREASON.

TALK TO OUR LEGAL DEPARTMENT.

COULD I OPT FOR THE EXECUTION INSTEAD?

THE COMPANY LAWYER

I'M WORKING ON A TOP SECRET MILITARY PROJECT. MY BOSS HIRED SOME NORTH ELBONIANS TO HELP ME.

THEY'RE COMMUNISTS. IF I GIVE THEM ANY INFORMATION, I COULD BE GUILTY OF TREASON. I COULD BE EXECUTED.

CAN YOU HELP?

SURE. WHAT WOULD I HAVE TO DO — PULL A LEVER?

DON'T WORRY THAT WE'LL TAKE ANY MILITARY TECHNOLOGY SECRETS BACK TO NORTH ELBONIA.

WE SIGNED THESE LITTLE AGREEMENTS THAT SAY WE WON'T.

HA HA HA HA HA!!

MOVING ON...

MY PROJECT HAS HIT A LITTLE SNAG.

OUR NORTH ELBONIAN CONTRACTORS STOLE OUR MILITARY TECHNOLOGY FOR THEIR BELLIGERENT HOMELAND. THEY'RE BUILDING A HUGE LASER TO VAPORIZE US.

NEXT YEAR, REMIND ME TO INCLUDE CONTRACT EMPLOYEES IN THE TEAM-BUILDING WORKSHOP.

THE FLOOR IS WARM!

... THE NORTH ELBONIANS STOLE OUR MILITARY TECHNOLOGY. WE THINK THEY'RE BUILDING A HUGE LASER TO USE AGAINST US.

ASK TINA THE TECH WRITER TO CREATE A USER MANUAL FOR THEM. REMIND TINA HOW THE NORTH ELBONIANS TREAT WOMEN.

LATER IN NORTH ELBONIA

OKAY... THE TIMER IS SET... WE'RE LINED UP IN SINGLE FILE... NOW WE SING A HELEN REDDY SONG.

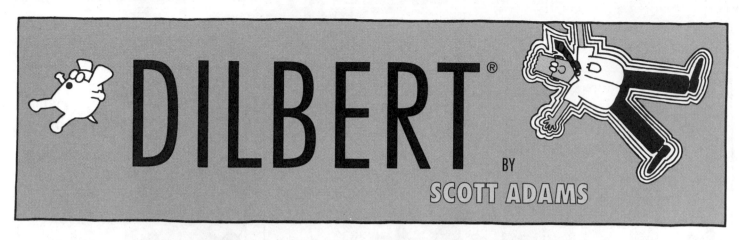

DILBERT®

BY **SCOTT ADAMS**

MAKING SOUP IS EASY FOR A HIGHLY TRAINED ENGINEER.

I DON'T SEEM TO HAVE ANY "COARSE SEA SALT."

I'LL JUST MIX REGULAR SALT WITH WATER.

CORN STARCH...HMM... THAT'S BASICALLY FLOUR.

MARJORAM... I THINK THAT'S FRENCH FOR BUTTER.

"FIVE INCHES OF PARMIGIANO-REGGIANO CHEESE RIND."

UH-OH.

EGGS ARE BASICALLY CHEESE THAT COMES FROM CHICKENS.

IS THIS SUPPOSED TO BE SERVED HOT?

YOU'RE THINKING OF GAZPACHO.

217

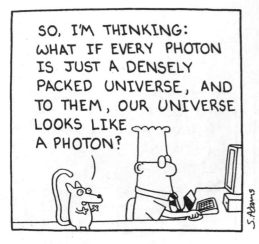

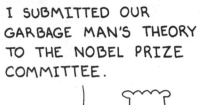

I SUBMITTED OUR GARBAGE MAN'S THEORY TO THE NOBEL PRIZE COMMITTEE.

I HOPE I WROTE THE THEORY RIGHT. I DON'T KNOW SHORTHAND SO I USED PIG LATIN TO SAVE TIME.

NOBEL PRIZE COMMITTEE

WHAT'S AN "OTON-PHAY"?

I LOVE WHAT YOU'RE DOING WITH YOUR HAIR.

NOBEL PRIZE COMMITTEE

OKAY, WE'VE NARROWED IT DOWN TO THE THEORIES WE DON'T UNDERSTAND.

IN SCIENCE, THE SIMPLEST SOLUTION IS USUALLY THE BEST. WHICH OF THESE THEORIES IS THE SIMPLEST SOLUTION?

WELL... THAT WOULD BE WHATEVER IS ON TOP OF THE PILE.

ARE WE SURE WE CAN'T VOTE FOR OURSELVES?

NOW THAT YOU'VE WON THE NOBEL PRIZE, I GUESS YOU'LL LEAVE THE GARBAGE INDUSTRY.

NO.

I'D MISS THE ACTION. I'D MISS THE SMELLS... THE SIGHTS... THE PEOPLE...

...THE RATS.

I ACCIDENTALLY THREW OUT A PAPER PLATE LAST WEEK. WOULD YOU LOOK FOR IT?

I'M KIDDING ABOUT THE PEOPLE PART.

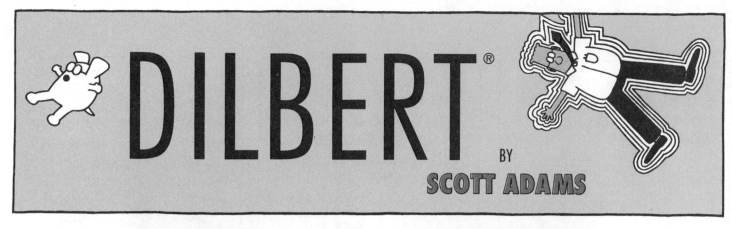

DILBERT ® BY SCOTT ADAMS

Dilbert: I'LL NEVER GET DRUNK. I DON'T WANT TO BE OUT OF CONTROL.

Dogbert: ARE YOU IN CONTROL AT WORK?

Dilbert: WELL... NO.

Dogbert: ARE YOU IN CONTROL WHEN YOU'RE ON A DATE?

Dilbert: I CAN'T GET A DATE.

Dilbert: AND WHOSE IDEA WAS IT TO GO ON THIS WALK?

Dogbert: YOURS.

Dilbert: ARE YOU SAYING I SHOULD GET DRUNK?

Dogbert: NO, NO.

Dogbert: I'M SAYING THE DECISION WILL BE MADE BY THE BEER COMPANIES.

Dilbert: I HOPE THEY SAY IT'S OKAY.

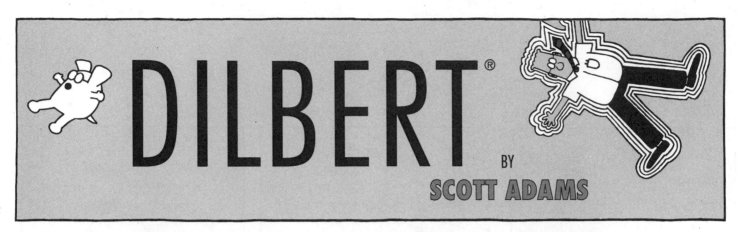

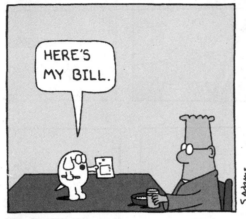

YOU TOO CAN EXPERIENCE THE PLEASURE OF CRUEL EMPLOYEE MANIPULATION. C'MON, TRY IT YOU BIG WUSS!

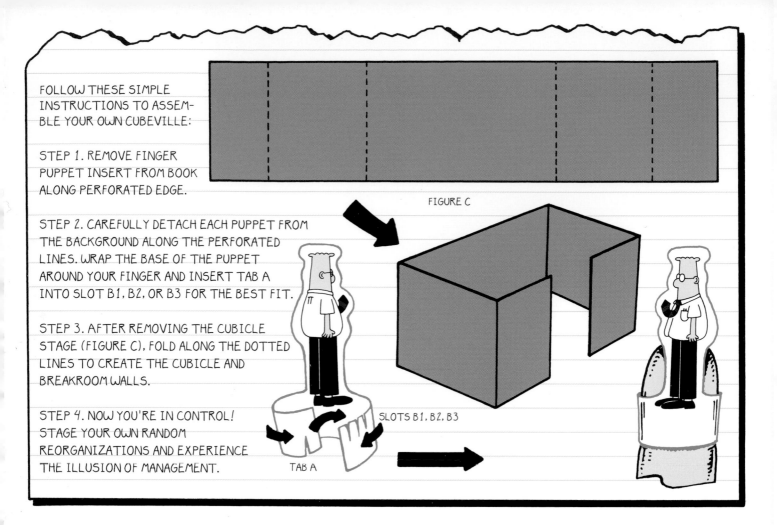

FOLLOW THESE SIMPLE INSTRUCTIONS TO ASSEMBLE YOUR OWN CUBEVILLE:

STEP 1. REMOVE FINGER PUPPET INSERT FROM BOOK ALONG PERFORATED EDGE.

STEP 2. CAREFULLY DETACH EACH PUPPET FROM THE BACKGROUND ALONG THE PERFORATED LINES. WRAP THE BASE OF THE PUPPET AROUND YOUR FINGER AND INSERT TAB A INTO SLOT B1, B2, OR B3 FOR THE BEST FIT.

STEP 3. AFTER REMOVING THE CUBICLE STAGE (FIGURE C), FOLD ALONG THE DOTTED LINES TO CREATE THE CUBICLE AND BREAKROOM WALLS.

STEP 4. NOW YOU'RE IN CONTROL! STAGE YOUR OWN RANDOM REORGANIZATIONS AND EXPERIENCE THE ILLUSION OF MANAGEMENT.

FIGURE C

SLOTS B1, B2, B3

TAB A

© UFS, Inc.